FIND
YOUR"
VOICE

FIND YOUR "VOICE"

CAROLINE GOYDER

Vermilion
LONDON

1 3 5 7 9 10 8 6 4 2

Published in 2020 by Vermilion an imprint of Ebury Publishing,
20 Vauxhall Bridge Road,
London SW1V 2SA

Vermilion is part of the Penguin Random House group of companies
whose addresses can be found at global.penguinrandomhouse.com

Penguin
Random House
UK

First published by Vermilion in 2020

www.penguin.co.uk

A CIP catalogue record for this book is available from the British Library

ISBN 9781785042836

Printed and bound in Great Britain by Clays Ltd, Elcograf S.p.A.

MIX
Paper from
responsible sources
FSC
www.fsc.org   FSC® C018179

Penguin Random House is committed to a
sustainable future for our business, our readers
and our planet. This book is made from Forest
Stewardship Council® certified paper.

To

my parents who gave me love of voice and sound (with a background of jazz saxophone). And to my girls who remind me of it every day.

You cannot think of the voice apart from the person; it is the person speaking ... The voice is a statement of yourself – it is 'I am', physically part of your whole self.

Cicely Berry, *Your Voice and How to Use it Successfully* (1990)

———————

Voice

1. The sound produced in a person's larynx and uttered through the mouth, as speech or song
1.1 The ability to speak or sing
1.2 The supposed utterance of a guiding spirit
1.3 The distinctive style or tone of a literary work or author

2. An agency by which a point of view is expressed or represented
2.1 The right to express an opinion

Oxford English Dictionary

———————

Contents

CONTENTS

Introduction

They weren't much older than she was and already they
had a voice . . . she wondered how they'd gotten it?

MEG WOLITZER, *THE FEMALE PERSUASION* (2018)

Your voice isn't 'lost'. You haven't left it on a train seat or
under the cushions on your sofa. It is with you now; you
just have to know where to find it. Put your hand on your
stomach and laugh. Feel that? Your voice is right there, deep
in your torso; buried treasure. It's always been there. And
what's always been there is harder to appreciate. That's both
the wonder of it, and the challenge. At your birth, a midwife
listened carefully to your voice to rate your health as a new-
born, as part of the Apgar score test, assessing the health of
your lungs communicated on your first cry.[1] From your very
first breath and that first cry that followed it, to the very last
breath you take, your voice is the bridge between your inner
life and the world out there.

Two young fish are swimming along in a river when they
meet an older fish. 'Morning boys,' he says as he passes, 'how's
the water?' The two young fish swim on in puzzled silence
until one glances over to the other and says, 'What the hell is

1

water?' As the writer David Foster Wallace comments on this story: 'the most obvious, ubiquitous, important realities are the ones we don't talk about.'[2] Voice is one of those obvious, ubiquitous, important realities; we don't talk about it, even as it enables us to talk. That is until it shakes, or squeaks or sounds weird on a video.

So, take a moment to notice your voice. Pay attention. Attention gives you control. And control ultimately gives you confidence. Talk to me. Say something. Read this out if you like. It's fine to speak quietly. I don't mind. Why not put a hand in front of your mouth as you speak? Feel how the air flows out of your lungs. Feel it vibrate on your larynx. Feel the warmth of the vibrating air molecules touch your hand as you speak. Feel your voice travelling out of you to meet the wide world. Notice for a moment this little miracle, what the writer Al Alvarez described as the 'expression of your aliveness'.[3]

Breath is life. Voice is breath. Your voice *is you*. When you can say 'This is my voice', you find that the world sits up and listens because you communicate from a place that is strong and clear. You speak up with confidence. You stand out.

When Words Fail You

Confidence comes from the Latin word *confidere* – meaning to trust. But how can you trust yourself when your words fail you just at the moment you need them most? How can you trust yourself if your voice is shaking? Or if you go blank in the spotlight of an audience's attention? Or if people always have to ask you to speak up because they can't hear you? Or if you worry that your voice is too soft, too loud, too high, too low, too much? How can you trust yourself if you can't trust your own voice?

If this all sounds familiar, welcome to the club. When I ask audiences, who has experienced a deficit of confidence as a speaker, it's normal for most hands to go up. Most people will tell you that deep down they feel vulnerable in what my drama school teacher described as 'hell's-mouth-opening' moments in front of an audience, or a camera, or a microphone.

These are some of the most feared moments:

- You step out in front of a large audience and they look at you expectantly.
- You want to speak up, but the room is full of experts. You feel stupid.
- You want to ask a question but feel your heart pounding in your chest and you worry your voice will shake.
- Someone asks you a question and everyone goes silent. You can't think of an answer.
- You have a camera pointed in your face and you have to say something intelligent off the cuff.

You can probably draw on any number of these moments in your memory. Seared into my brain is the memory of a stage in a huge hall where I went badly wrong in front of a thousand people. I vowed afterwards that I would never speak on stage again. It took me a while to rebuild my confidence. It still makes me cringe to think about it now. Though you can feel very alone in those moments, you really aren't. This fear is human. Nerves are normal. On a daily basis, clients recount memories of embarrassment, fear and vulnerability as speakers. And I hear these stories from all ages, from schoolchildren to people who run global businesses and lead countries. For example, an executive told me that she remembers the moment she stepped up to give a speech at school, no notes in hand as her dad told her to learn it by heart. She forgot her words and everyone laughed. She decided that speaking was risky and that belief followed her for years in a highly successful career.

But though these moments connect us all, so does our capacity to learn from them and to improve. The executive can now say – with quiet pride – that many years on from her school disaster she has graced stages in front of thousands of people feeling in control, enjoying the experience. Hand on heart I can tell you that speaking with confidence is learned not innate. There's no such thing as a 'born' speaker. It's what you do, day in, day out, that makes you confident, not who you are. For 30 years I wasn't a confident speaker. I rushed. I shook. I worried. But steadily, using the steps I'm going to show you, I found that my confidence as a speaker grew.

The word 'abracadabra', that old favourite of magicians pulling rabbits out of hats, actually comes from the Hebrew *'ebrah k'dabri'*, meaning 'I will create as I speak'. Finding your voice is a kind of magic. The moment you feel the easy power of your voice release from deep in your body. The moment you discover you have the power to walk out in the spotlight and find your way home to calm, no matter what. To know your voice won't shake. To know that you can harness the adrenalin rather than dread it. To know when you need to fill a room, there's no need to shout.

As a speaker I started to find a new normal which allowed me to feel calm and controlled when I spoke. I found that I could step up to stages and audiences that felt daunting and handle the situation. And as a teacher I relish the moment when voices transform like plants unfurling in a summer garden. It makes my job a joy. And I want you to flourish in the same way too. When you handle these moments well, doors open. Word gets around. Your life changes. And when you are speaking up for ideas bigger than you, you change the lives of others too. And that's where it gets really interesting.

MADE NOT BORN

If you want an example of a confident speaker who was made not born, look no further than the ancient world's role model for overcoming voice impediments – Demosthenes. Born in Athens in 384 BC, Demosthenes was not a 'natural' speaker. He was physically weak as a child and had a bad stutter. His first attempts at speaking in public were a disaster – he was jeered out of the assembly. But he was determined. He set out to find his voice. He put pebbles in his mouth to help him speak clearly (don't try this at home . . .), he practised in front of a shield polished up as a mirror, he ran up hills to strengthen his lungs. His confidence and his voice grew until he became one of the most respected speakers of his time.

Your Voice Matters More than Ever

There's never been a better time to learn to speak with confidence. The unintended consequence of our technological age is that the voice – the real human voice – matters more than ever. Even the techies agree: the message coming out of Silicon Valley is that human communication matters even more than code. LinkedIn CEO, Jeff Weiner, believes that oral communication is one of the key skills gaps of the future. As he said at a *Wired* forum on the future of work: 'As powerful as AI will ultimately become and is becoming, we're still a ways away from computers being able to replicate and replace human interaction and human touch. So there's a wonderful incentive for people to develop these skills.'[4]

When computers can do most things faster than humans, it is the ultra-human skills that will allow us to stand out. Wouldn't a good outcome of the rise of AI be that humans become more humane? And voice is the core of what makes us human because it allows us to communicate intricate shifts, moment by moment, as a response to what is happening right in front of us, and deep within us. No machine can replicate that.

And if speaking matters now, know this: your ability to speak and to influence others is only going to become more important in the future. This trajectory has been tracked. In 1995, the American economist Deirdre McCloskey led a significant study covering 140 million people in the USA that analysed 250 different occupations.[5] She wanted to know how much time people spent presenting to others, and persuading them to change their minds. McCloskey's findings were that the importance of speaking was rising fast and that persuasion would represent 40 per cent of the value of America's national income in the next 20 years (so by 2015). In her conclusion, McCloskey commented on the importance of the voice as a tool for persuasion: 'Nothing happens voluntarily in an economy or a society unless someone changes their mind. Behaviour can be changed by compulsion, but minds cannot.'

McCloskey's thesis was tested again when the study was reviewed in 2013 in Australia. The Australian Treasury study found that persuasion had in fact risen to 30 per cent of US GDP.[6] And if Jeff Weiner is correct in his assertion of the importance of human communication, that figure is likely to continue to rise. It may soon hit the 40 per cent value that the 1995 study predicted.

That's why it's my belief that voice is the ultimate human soft power. In a political sense 'soft power',[7] the term coined by political scientist Joseph S. Nye to describe a nation's power to attract and persuade, is the opposite of 'hard power', with its implications of the use of might. On an individual level, hard and soft power exist too. Your job title, or your place in the world, offers a kind of positional hard power. But it only takes you so far. It's the infinite variety of your voice, its empathy, emotion and nuance, that gives you the ability to influence. This is a different kind of soft power and it matters more than ever.

The Confidence Catch-22 of the Digital Age

If you want to speak with confidence now, what you must understand is that there's a new obstacle to finding your voice, a toxic digital Catch-22. So many different platforms exist on which to share your voice with a global audience: podcasts, YouTube channels, social media and who knows what next. But every silver lining has a cloud. Platforms can bring performance pressure. Want to be a YouTube sensation? Then first you'll have to overcome the anxiety that makes you look nervous and twitchy on camera. Podcasts are a challenge if you hate your voice. That video call is going to be a problem if you are worried about not knowing when to speak. The age of video is a golden age of opportunity for you to make your voice heard, but only if that voice doesn't wobble when you press record.

To this toxic mix of platforms and pressure we can also add a lack of practice when it comes to using our voices. Speaking can sometimes seem like a dying art – the tongue superseded by typing fingers. My grandparents, who died in the 1990s, would have been astonished by human behaviour today: constantly checking our devices, peering into our phones as we walk down the street. They would wonder why on earth we would message someone when they are just a few desks away or in the next room. They would remark on offices that have become silent spaces, punctuated only by tapping keys. They would find it hard to believe that work relationships can be mediated without speech. They might notice that the little boxes we use to communicate have actually boxed us in. They would be staggered by the pace at which we try to keep up with our devices, careering through our lives without stopping to breathe, to connect, to be present for others. We hide silently behind screens for most of our lives. It's no surprise that if you put yourself out there on the global digital stage – on a podcast or on YouTube – and you haven't been using your voice much and you haven't practised, you are bound to experience anxiety. Over time these moments knock our confidence.

At the same time as the world of work becomes a more silent place, many of us are actively getting into habits which make confident speaking harder. All the texting and emailing and leaning over screens has a big impact on our physical selves. People speak faster, with shoulders tensed, eyes glazed and with shallow breathing. At precisely the same time as our modern media requires that we are totally natural, unwaveringly individual, our gadgets are making it harder to do when we speak. Have you ever wondered if all that swiping and scrolling is making you worse at getting your words out calmly and coherently? Just think about it now: you look at your phone with your head down; notice your breath, is it shallow and are you holding it? Your focus is inwards, rather than out into the world around you.

When pressure meets a lack of practice it creates paranoia. Think of one of those moments in life where external pressure meets the stress created by your devices. Used to peering into a screen, hunched over, your body is far more likely to interpret an audience that is looking at you as a threat. Your stressed system labels the rush as bad. Frightening. Dangerous, even. And your system raises the alarm: your heart rate rises, your blood races to the heart and limbs. You get speedy, you rush or you fluster and mumble. Or worse, you go blank.

The good news? With a little awareness of the impact our devices can have, this is all infinitely avoidable. And that's what mindfulness is designed to help us to do, right? Well, yes and no. Mindfulness is wonderful and will help enormously. But there's a missing link. The Tibetan Buddhists don't talk of mind–body–spirit; they talk of *mind–body–voice*. And we need to create this link between the mind, body and voice. That's what this book is about. I want you to feel in control, not just *before* you speak, but *when* you speak. And, more than that, I want you to learn that it is possible to actually calm yourself down *as* you speak, so that you don't ever have to feel like a runaway train. And in the digital age there is more reason than ever before to find your voice.

How this Book Works

When we plant a rose seed in the earth, we notice that it is small, but we do not criticize it as 'rootless and stemless'. We treat it as a seed, giving it the water and nourishment required of a seed ... Within it at all times, it contains its whole potential. It seems to be constantly in the process of change; yet at each stage, at each moment, it is perfectly all right as it is.

W. Timothy Gallwey, *The Inner Game of Tennis* (1975)

I have a belief that if you can chat with confidence to your friends, you can speak with confidence to a thousand people. If you can speak calmly and confidently in front of one audience, you can do it anywhere. You're using the same instrument. The question is how you access confidence under pressure.

That's why this book is about unlocking the confidence already within you. And the key to that confidence is in awareness and then practice.

I'm a voice coach. Day in, day out I help people to step up and speak in pitches, in video conferences, on big stages, in meeting rooms, at parties, on podcasts. And what I see over and over again is that when you get some practical skills deep in the muscle, through practice, your confidence opens up. Twenty years of doing the little things on a daily basis has changed my ability to speak with confidence. That's why I want you to get excited about the magic of little and often. In this book I will teach you to become more aware of your voice and then give you simple practices to apply little and often so you can speak with more and more confidence. Trust the process, commit to it and your voice and your confidence will unfold in ways that will surprise and delight you.

Aristotle had a word for this potential of things to become themselves – entelechy. It is a compound of the Greek word *en* (within), *telos* (moving towards) and *ekhein* (to be in a certain state). Just as the acorn becomes the oak when the conditions are right, so you already contain within you every-thing you need to speak with confidence.

I see over and over again that with the right care, watering and attention your voice will flourish. Voice is a force of nature. And nature is resourceful. When the right conditions are in place she will do the rest. My father-in-law has spent many years creating and tending his arboretum in Scotland. Trees from all over the world grow on his hillside, rippling in the bracing wind off the Trossachs. Walking up the hill one winter's morning he pointed to what looked to my untrained eye like a stick in the ground. 'That's an incredibly rare Chinese tree,' he said. He'd bought it on his travels and planted it in the rich Scotch earth only for it to disappear. He thought he'd killed it until it pushed up again through the earth one spring, next to its metal sign. It was always there, waiting, potent. When the conditions were right, it reappeared. The entelechy of this Chinese tree was there in the soil. It was just waiting until the conditions were right. You are the same. Your ability to speak with confidence is there, waiting to spring up. You simply have to create the right conditions for your mind–body–voice to flourish – how you think, how you stand, how you breathe.

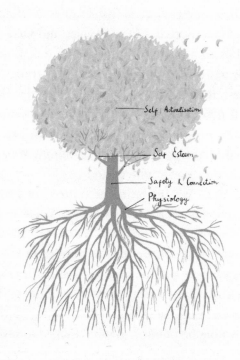

When it comes to creating the right conditions that will allow you to speak with confidence, you can't do better than follow the psychologist Abraham Maslow's famous hierarchy of needs, shown in the form of a tree here. We follow this system in this book, as it provides the perfect conditions to help you to care for and nurture your voice so you can speak with confidence. Each level of the Maslow tree reflects a pattern of growth which leads us to expressing our potential, finding meaning, finding our voice. In each of these levels we can find skills which will help us to speak with confidence.

In Chapter One Your Incredible Instrument, we look at how your voice works. When you understand what is happening, you are already more in control. And there's a whole 'root system' of your voice that you may never have considered. Hidden away in the depths of your torso is the powerhouse of your voice. It may be out of sight, but I want it to be firmly in your awareness.

In Chapter Two Find Your Calm Centre, we climb from the roots of physiology to the trunk of safety needs. If we can't find safety we will feel anxious and fearful when we speak. This chapter shows you what to do when you feel scared or anxious, and your voice shakes. This trunk of your calm centre also allows you to access the next part of Maslow's hierarchy. Calm helps you to find safety and safety helps you to feel you are with friends. That's when as a speaker you can move up to connection or love and belonging – the next level in Maslow's hierarchy. Connection is something we can generate from within if we know how. It's essential to speaking with confidence because when you see the audience as friends you can relax and have fun as a speaker. It removes at a stroke the unpleasant feeling of being at the mercy of a judgemental audience. You can switch it on for yourself even when you are alone in the spotlight in front of a thousand people.

The next level of Maslow's hierarchy is esteem – the desire for competence and achievement. These are the branches of the tree, allowing you to open up and speak with confidence. We look at how to set up the physical conditions for esteem in Chapter Three Get Out of Your Head: How to Embody Confidence When You Speak via your posture and awareness so that you can show up feeling confident before you speak. It creates a virtuous circle where people respect you as being confident and so your confidence grows.

Finally we move up to the top of the tree – the leaves – self-actualisation. This is where you express your individual voice fully. In Chapter Four Speak Up Stand Out we focus on how you self-actualise and express your ideas confidently, rather than censoring yourself.

Each stage builds one on top of the other and as you become more confident you will find that the next layer of the hierarchy opens up for you. Plant deep roots, give the right care and feeding, create the right conditions and watch your voice and confidence flourish.

Your Questions

At the end of most chapters you will find questions that I get asked a lot. These are real people's questions, from 20 years of helping people to speak with confidence. At the beginning of my sessions, we talk about the moment of fear when we have to find our voices. I ask everyone to write their questions and fears on sticky notes and we put them all up on the wall. It's incredibly cathartic for everyone to hear how normal these fears are, whether senior or junior in a company, or an experienced or beginner speaker. We *all* have the same fears about our voices.

Common Questions

How do I stay calm in the spotlight?

How can I stop feeling anxious, knowing I have to speak?

How do I calm down/regain control once I've started speaking?

How do I get a more interesting tone in my voice when speaking?

How do I stop feeling intimidated?

How do I not waffle and say 'um' and 'er' a lot?

How do I stop my hands shaking?

How do I have the confidence to speak up in meetings and feel confident when lots of people are talking?

How do I learn to ask questions without worrying that people are judging me?

How to Get the Most from this Book

A book cannot, in itself, open up your voice and help you to speak with confidence, any more than a book can make a cake for you. Speaking, like cooking or gardening, takes love and practice, and a little each day moves you forward as the days accumulate. I know this because I've lived it. Someone commented recently that they loved my voice. It caught me by surprise because for years I felt frustrated and let down by my voice. Twenty years ago, if you'd told me then that I would enjoy my voice now, I'm not sure I would have believed you. So what made the difference? I put the work in. The more regularly you practise, lightly, little and often, the more your voice and confidence will open up.

For too long to mention, I was the voice coach who knew the exercises theoretically but didn't do them. We are all full of good intentions and then life gets in the way. But about a decade ago, I found the exercises that worked for me, that slotted into my life, and that was when everything changed. This is what I want you to take from this book: commit five minutes of your day, each day, ideally in the morning, to your voice, because that is what I had to do. This will set your voice up for the day. Choose the exercises and advice that work for you from this book, make them a habit and then get addicted to how your voice opens up and the impact this gives you in the world.

That's why I want you to get stuck in: fold pages, write notes, try the exercises. Go away and think about what you've read, mull it over, then make it yours. Come back, read another section, try it, test it, 'get it in the muscle' as we say in the acting world! As such, this book is deliberately structured into short sections.

This book is about what you *do*. If you only remember one thing when it comes to the voice, remember this: consistency beats intensity every time. Consistency builds new habits deep into the muscle and allows you to be instinctive when you are in front of your audience, just like when you learn to drive, you practise consistently so you can be instinctive in the test. You need to find one or more of the techniques that feel easy and practical enough to do every day.

Finding your voice is about taking small steps, one foot in front of the other. Do it and trust the process. When you get fit, you trust that you can move more and fitness will follow. If you believe you are unfit and never walk anywhere, nothing will change. Consistency of the five-minutes-a-day kind can change your voice faster than you realise.

Throughout the book you will find **Try This exercises** which you can use to get an understanding of the concepts and techniques of voice training. Try them all, find the exercises that work for you and find the right moments each day for a few minutes of practice. When you do these exercises depends very much on the structure of your day. The morning may work if you have a nine-to-five life in an office. If I am going to be out at work all day, I do them in the morning before I leave and find that the confidence and calm stays with me all day. But some clients top up their confidence throughout the day, they might take themselves off to a quiet meeting room for five minutes before a meeting. If you work from home, as so many people do now, you may have much more flexibility as to when you do these exercises. Perhaps you are speaking at an event in the evening, so you might get home and do them as you get ready. Simply trust your instinct as to what works for you. But whatever you do, find the time to practise. If you simply read this book nothing will change. And do what you enjoy, as then you will stick to it. Not everything appeals to everyone. That's totally normal and totally okay. What I know deeply from my work is that people find different exercises useful. I suggest you try everything once and then collect what resonantes for you so that you can 'get it into the muscle'.

Keep these principles in mind to help you enjoy the process:

Keep it simple: My advice is to work through this book bit by bit, just like a cookery book. Take an idea that appeals. Try it, taste it, feel it, get it into the body, breath and voice and, when it's yours, come back and try something else. Experiment with simple, powerful ways in which you can explore the power of your voice.

Create new habits: Little and often is what matters. Voices open up when you give them gentle, easy, enjoyable repetition. Find a way to do the exercises during activities you already do, such as making coffee in the morning, getting dressed, commuting, reading to your children. Doing something daily, for five minutes, wins out every time over doing something for an hour, every so often.

Be light: If you force a seat belt too hard, it locks. Trying too hard to find your voice has the same effect. We learn at school to work hard at things. We furrow our brows, set our jaws, try really hard. But that doesn't work for voice because it puts tension into the system. And tension locks down your voice and blocks your confidence. Voice is a physical thing – and when we tense up nothing flows. It's the same as dancing, tennis, art. Overthink it and you won't succeed. Relax, lighten up and you will find everything flows. Aldous Huxley put it well in his 1962 novel *Island* – 'It's dark because you are trying too hard. Lightly child, lightly. Learn to do everything lightly.'

Be curious: What you think you know has layers and layers to explore. That is true of voice. You may know how to speak – I felt I did 20 years ago – but two decades later, after exploring day in day out, I feel I'm just getting started. Come at the exercises and ideas in this book with what a martial arts expert calls a 'beginner's mind'. It's a great learning state; the freshness and curiosity it gives you will even allow you to experience things you thought you already knew in a different light.

'No daylight on magic,' said the photographer Cecil Beaton. Test these exercises out at home and allow them to feel comfortable and natural before you take them out into the world. You don't have to tell anyone about it. Just let them notice in time.

Success after reading this book will be that when you have five minutes – it could be at the start of the day, before a meeting, a moment where you feel anxious – you will know exactly what to do in that time to help you speak with confidence.

I HATE 'PUBLIC SPEAKING'

This might surprise you but I would ban the expression 'public speaking'. It makes something perfectly normal to you – speaking, chatting – sound highly unnatural and worrying. Words have power and I want you to feel that speaking in front of an audience is just another part of the speaking you do every day. We don't say 'public dancing', 'public playing' and 'public singing' do we? Can we put 'public speaking' in Room 101 and agree to call it just 'speaking' from now on? Or even 'chatting'? Let's not put public speaking on a pedestal, or worse behind a lectern: I'd ban those too; they are where good speeches go to die.

CHAPTER ONE

Your Incredible Instrument

Voice: something that begins around the back of the
knees and reaches well above the head.

PHILIP ROTH, *THE GHOST WRITER* [1979]

You already know how to speak confidently. There are moments in your life, with the people you trust, where you speak with absolute ease and confidence. And it's my belief that if you can find your voice in those moments, you can find it in any situation.

The first step is to understand how the instrument of your voice works. In this chapter we are in Maslow's first level of physiology – your foundations/roots. I'm going to take you on a tour of the hidden power of your incredible instrument. When you understand how your voice works you discover that, in the words of the director and playwright Peter Brook, there are 'drawers in the self' filled with everything you need to speak with confidence. This power within was symbolised in a TEDx talk I did by a large chest of drawers shaped like a man's torso, called Big Ted.[1] When you understand how your voice works you will realise that:

- Speaking can be simple.
- You don't have to rush as a speaker because you know how to centre your breath with the diaphragm.
- You no longer have people telling you to speak up because you can project from your deep core muscles.
- When you trip over your words you know how to find clarity in the articulators.

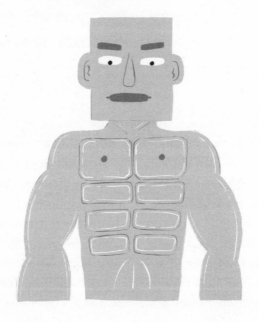

Let's take a tour of different aspects of the instrument so that you can draw on them in each chapter. And of course, you can refer back to this chapter at any time if you need a reminder.

How Your Voice Works

During my TEDx talk, I took a small guitar from one of the drawers in Big Ted. Using a guitar is a good way to explain the instrument of the voice: a guitar has *strings*; the *hitter* which vibrates the strings; and the *body* resonates the sound. The instrument of your voice is similar: it has strings – your *vocal folds*; there is a hitter – the *air/breath* that comes out of your lungs, supported by the muscles of the body; there is a resonator – your *body*. Voice production, or phonation, works a bit like a guitar. Air flows out of the lungs, hits the strings of the vocal folds, which vibrate, then the body resonates the sound. This creates voice. The final stage of speech is where the comparison with the guitar stops – as speech then requires the speech muscles, the articulators, to shape it.

In this section I want to take you on a guided tour of the main parts of your instrument:

- The **strings** - your *vocal folds*
- The **hitter** - your *breath*
- The **resonator** - your *body*
- The **articulators** - your *lips and tongue, assisted by a relaxed jaw and energised facial muscles*

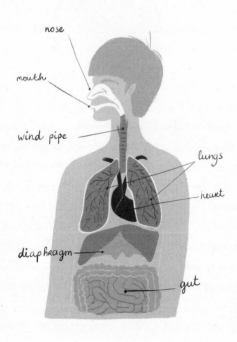

The reason to take the instrument apart is so that you understand the anatomy and know how to react and what to adjust in moments of stress. Sometimes you just need to do one small thing to make a difference and you can only know what to do when you understand how each part of your voice works in isolation.

THE SURPRISING SECRET TO SPEAKING WITH CONFIDENCE

Speaking doesn't have to be stressful. When you understand the instrument, speaking can calm you down. The key is breathing. Voice is breath. And breathing is the master key to the nervous system. The neuroscientist Antonio Damasio explains that though 'We are about as effective at stopping an emotion as we are at preventing a sneeze', there is one area of our nervous system we can control: 'One partial exception to the extremely limited control we have . . . concerns respiratory control, over which we need to exert some voluntary action, because autonomic respiration and voluntary vocalisation for speech and singing use the same instrument.'[2]

We breathe to live and to speak. And so when you are aware of how the voice works, and in particular the interplay between voice and breath, then you start to develop a very fine degree of awareness over the nervous system.

The Strings: Your Vocal Folds

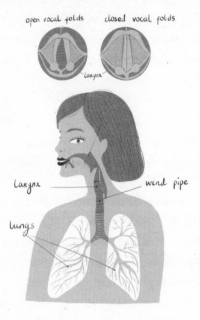

Let's start with the strings of your instrument. All sound is a change in air pressure. To create sound in the instrument of your voice you have strings and a hitter to create this change in pressure. Your vocal folds are the muscular strings of your instrument. These vocal folds, or cords as you may know them, are a system of muscles set within the cartilage of the larynx. Air pressure is the hitter in the voice and it needs extra power for speech than for normal breathing.

So, how does this hitter of air pressure create sound? When we speak, air flows out of the lungs and the vocal folds vibrate by closing and opening at top speed. If you want to understand how they work it can help to think of a balloon pulled open to let the air out and the sound that results. As air leaves the lungs it forces the vocal folds apart. A drop in pressure enables the vocal folds to shut and then the air from the lungs forces the folds to open again. The folds open and close very quickly in response to this. When your exhaled breath meets the vocal folds the air pressure forces them open and closed very quickly creating a vibration. This vibration is *voice*. Volume in voice is air pressure – the larger the air pressure change, the bigger the sound. Go on to YouTube and search for 'vocal folds singing' and you can see this process in action, as singers sing with a camera down their throat. It's well worth taking a look.[3]

The pitch of your voice is a result of the tension in the vocal folds. If the folds are relaxed, not stretched out, the pitch is lower. When the folds are long and stretched, with more tension, the pitch is higher.

Try This: Find Your Vocal Folds

I want you to get to know your vocal folds so that you can understand how to care for them. Essentially the more you can take the effort and work away from the throat and allow the body to be the powerhouse, the more the voice opens up. These explorations will help you to recognise how your voice works, as you try out a few sounds.

1. Say 'aaaa' as you do at the doctor's (it's a nice open sound, but you can play with pretty much any vowel).

Put a hand on your larynx (what you will feel is the thyroid cartilage that sits at the front of the voice box, you can't feel the vocal folds themselves). As you say 'aaaa' feel it vibrate. That's a *voiced* sound.

2. Now say 'ssh' or 'sssssss' or 'fff' and feel that there's no vibration on the larynx. Instead the sound is produced by friction between the tongue and the roof of the mouth, or the lips and teeth. These are *voiceless* sounds.

3. If you say a high 'iii' sound, your vocal folds become thin and elongated, like a stretched rubber band. If you say a low 'ooo' sound, the folds are thicker, less elongated, like a looser rubber band.

4. Now see if you can find a really low sound, as low as you can go saying 'haa'. Let it be easy. This is *creak* – your vocal folds at their most relaxed. You may feel your larynx drop as you do this.

5. Finally do a glide from somewhere at the top of your range to the bottom on 'mee' or 'hee'. If you put your fingers on your larynx at the front you might feel that it moves up on high notes and down for low notes. You may notice if you put one hand on the top of your head and one hand on the stomach that the high notes buzz in the head and the lower notes resonate down the body. You can feel that what happens on your vocal folds has an impact through the whole body.

The Hitter: Your Breath

The jar of air/breath from my TEDx talk

The hitter for the voice is air. Exhaled air. We speak on an out-breath. It's strange to have to say it, but we think about voice so little that most people do need a reminder. Test it. Put your hand up to your mouth and say the days of the week. Feel the exhaled air on your hand. The air is going out isn't it? Now try speaking on an inhalation. Doesn't work does it? I know of two exceptions to this: the Xhosa in South Africa and Zimbabwe who speak with some inhaled clicks and the Norwegians do an inhaled '*Ja!*' for effect. There are more I'm sure – let me know if you're aware of any.

The Wave

When you sleep your body breathes for you. It doesn't need any conscious input at all. You can deduce from this that your body is pretty good at breathing without your help. The more you can get out of the way and let the reflex of your breath do its work, the better. The problem for most people when they speak to an audience is that they overdo things, losing their natural ease and instead becoming tense and talking too quickly.

The instrument doesn't work well when you force it. It works much better when you understand the power of a tidal breath. This is the reflex breath that your body naturally does when you get out of the way. You know how well it works because your body breathes really efficiently when you're asleep. When you are relaxed your breathing naturally replaces itself.

If you want to understand your breath, try this exercise. Go to the beach in your mind. Imagine the sights, smells and feelings of that beach. Imagine the waves coming in and going out, and focus on the rhythm of the waves. In – pause – out – pause is the rhythm of each wave as it comes into the beach. Notice how if you relax and observe your breath, it naturally reverts to the in – pause – out – pause rhythm. Breath is tidal, it has the same rhythm as a wave on a beach. A wave of breath comes in, a wave goes out. Your body functions on this wave power, all day, all night; through every moment of life your body breathes, your

> lungs and your heart are expanding and contracting. When you find that rhythm naturally you start to harness the energy of the breath in a way that will really power your voice. It's a highly renewable energy.

This natural rhythm is always there if you relax and let it happen. I recommend you do. Trust that your body knows how to breathe. Just look after the out-breath and then relax and let the body replace it with the in-breath in its own way. You don't have to pull it, there's a natural reflex that senses the need for oxygen and tells the body to breathe. Don't obsess about whether the breath is coming in through the nose or mouth.

When you breathe out notice the moment *after* the out-breath and *before* the next in-breath. For the body, this is a lovely moment of pause between the breath – a stillness. Air has flowed out of the lungs and the body is in a state of rest between the two forces of the in-breath and the out-breath (in- and out-breath cancel each other out). It is a moment without respiratory movement. It's a time when the body can stop and relax. If you ever need help to relax when trying to fall asleep, follow the out-breath all the way to the end and then let the body wait for the wave of in-breath to happen in its own time. Your body will start to relax. 'Feel a breath wanting to enter again', says the voice teacher, Kristin Linklater. 'And then all you do is yield to that need ... let it happen ... Let the air breathe you.'[4]

Try This: Feel the Reflex

You can do this sitting or standing. Place a hand on your stomach. Ground your feet on to the floor. Take your attention inside the body to your lungs, ribs and stomach muscles.

Inhale

Belly out

Exhale

Belly in

1. Breathe out as if blowing out candles on a birthday cake. Feel your stomach move towards the spine and the ribs close together like two bucket handles. Follow that out-breath all the way out as the lungs expel the air (though there's always a bit of breath left in the lungs).

2. Wait for the reflex. Notice that the body knows when to breathe in when you wait (just as it does when you are asleep).

3. When the body is ready to breathe in, feel the breath come in low and wide. Feel your stomach move away from the spine (think of a balloon opening the torso, front belly, side ribs, back ribs). Air comes in, is filtered by the nasal passages and sinuses and travels down the throat and windpipe. The ribs swing out and the lungs expand to draw in the breath. Air travels down the bronchial branches of the lungs into the tiny leaves of the alveoli (air sacs) before sending oxygen into the bloodstream. The diaphragm draws down as the breath comes in, moving the guts down.

4. Then blow out the birthday candles again. Feel the stomach squeeze back to the spine. Feel the breath go out. Feel the ribcage and lungs go back to their original shape. Feel the diaphragm flow back up again as the air flows out, expelling carbon dioxide from the bloodstream.

5. Now you have a sense of these lower muscles, can you feel them as you speak? Try speaking the days of the week. Feel how as you breathe in the stomach moves away from the spine, and as you speak the stomach moves back to the spine.

YOUR DAILY BREATH

In your daily life pay attention to the connection between your breath, your confidence and your voice. Notice how when you feel stressed and tense the breathing locks up into the upper body and notice how your thoughts become faster, more anxious. Notice that you can shift your thinking, and your emotion, by shifting the breath to the low and wide breath. Breathe low and wide whenever you remember – this is called pyramid breathing because it is wider at the bottom than at the top. And notice how your voice changes when you do. It becomes more relaxed, more confident. Notice how you feel more confident as a result. This is the key to harnessing your voice power. It is worth your consistent attention.

MEET YOUR POWER SOURCE: THE DIAPHRAGM

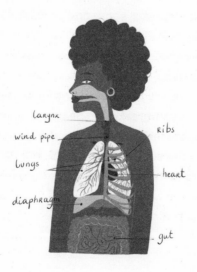

larynx

wind pipe

ribs

lungs

heart

diaphragm

gut

When we talk about the instrument of your voice, the *diaphragm* is the real power source. Speaking requires a powerful hitter and the important fact to understand is that the lungs have no muscle. They contain the air, but getting that air out of the body requires back-up; the lungs in themselves can't breathe. They need the diaphragm and intercostal muscles between the ribs to create space for breath to come in and to support the breath as it heads out of the body.

'Speak from the diaphragm' is very good advice. But it can seem a bit nebulous at first can't it? When people said the same thing to me I remember thinking, 'That sounds great, but what do they mean *exactly*? And how do I find my diaphragm? What does it even look like?'

Your diaphragm is essentially a sheet made of two domes and a central tendon. The thorax, the Latin word for shield, of the ribcage protects the diaphragm. Above the diaphragm is the thoracic cavity, the space created by the thorax. Above the diaphragm is air – the heart and lungs. Below it is the weightier, wetter world of your digestive system. Though the diaphragm is tucked away, nestled beneath the heart and lungs, you can get a sense of the front point of its attachment if you put your fingers at the front of your ribcage, at the base of your sternum. If you find the point just below your breast bone you can gently stick your thumb in and feel the front point of attachment of the diaphragm (just below your bra strap if you happen to be wearing one). Then you can track it round with your fingers as it attaches to the lower ribs at the sides and feel as it connects to your lumbar.

I love Jean Hall's description of the movement of the diaphragm in her book *Breathe*:

> Like a jellyfish with the tentacles reaching down as the two tendons (crura). Imagine the dome-shaped hood of a jellyfish opening and widening, and then closing and narrowing to propel itself upward through the water. Our diaphragm does the same: as we breathe in the crura tentacles contract, drawing the sheet of the diaphragm down towards the pelvis. This makes space for the lungs to expand, causing the belly to move outwards. As we breathe out the crura relax, which releases the diaphragm to float back up, pressing on the surface of the lungs which in turn expels the breath and allows the belly to recede.[5]

When your breathing is diaphragmatic, the whole of your expression feels joined up and you find that you move, speak and think in a calm, whole-system way. It makes body language – for example what to do with your hands – become redundant, because your whole system is moving as one. You no longer have to worry about separate pieces and begin to understand that the body only ever really works as one system. Thinking about body language is really just tinkering about at the edges. You want to get to the heart of things so you can work with the system as a whole. And the way into this is through the diaphragm. That is why the Ancient Greeks called this powerful double-dome-shaped muscle 'the unity of all possibilities of human expression'.

Jellyfish Breathing

This is a good exercise for whenever you have a few minutes to yourself, whether you're at home, on public transport on your way to a presentation, or waiting for a meeting. You can essentially do it whenever you have a moment. I trust you to find the right one.

There's a beautiful economy in breathing diaphragmatically. It calms the mind and body and centres the voice. In that sense this is the ultimate practice for speaking with confidence as the diaphragm is the key to your confidence. You can come back to this whenever you want to make contact with the diaphragm.

1. Imagine a jellyfish flowing down your body as you breathe in, and flowing back up the body carrying air out.

2. Feel the ribs swing back as you breathe in (the back of a chair can help you feel this, or you can put your hands on your ribs). Let the breath come in silently through the nose and feel the ribs swing out in your back, allowing the air to really drop into the lowest part of the lungs in your back. Notice the pause between the in-breath and the out-breath that we talked about on page 32. The breath comes in. The body waits. Then the breath flows out again. You don't have to do anything, just wait and observe that after your body breathes in, there is a pause and then the breath flows out of the body.

3. Trust your body to breathe. Trust the system. Let the air do its own thing at this point – either flowing in and out through the nose with a closed mouth, or letting the lips gently part so air can flow in and out through the mouth as well. Choose what allows you to feel at your most relaxed. Let the breath be easy. If it feels effortful or noisy, remind yourself that your body does this best when you are asleep, so the less that you try, the better this will work. Trust the body to do what it does best. Get out of the way. Relax. Observe. Feel the flow of the breath.

4. After a few minutes of jellyfish breathing, put a finger where the ribs separate at the front of the body and take note of how the point of attachment for your diaphragm at the front of the body has become soft (see page 38).

To keep this with you in life it can help to remind yourself to breathe low and wide down into the lower ribs rather than high and shallow into the upper chest.

BREATHE YOUR THOUGHTS AND EMOTIONS

We breathe out to speak. We breathe in to gather our thoughts. We refuel on pauses. They are imperceptible to an audience when done well because they are thinking about what you have just said. The Romans understood this, it's why the word 'inspiration' comes from the root '*spirare*', meaning 'to breathe'.

When you breathe diaphragmatically you 'infuse your words with spirit', to use a phrase from Maya Angelou. The heart and diaphragm nestle very closely to each other and studies have shown that the movement of the diaphragm provides an internal massage that assists the heart, even reducing the recurrence of heart attacks.[6] This heart–voice connection extends into language: those moments where we 'speak from the heart' are usually connected to a centred, diaphragmatic breath. Those speakers who engage their hearts as well as their minds, speak from this emotional centre. We remember what they make us feel, as much as what they say. Because *they* feel it first. This energy is exactly the quality our age craves – intimacy, vulnerability, the full human being rather than a locked-down version. It's there in any great speaker in the digital age – open, easy, expressive. And the most effective way to open up that energy is to let your body relax and let the jellyfish of the diaphragm move freely (see page 39) so you can connect to your feelings and let your voice express them in the right way to your audience.

Science is making the connection between emotions and breathing patterns. A 2002 study showed that different emotions are connected to specific breathing patterns.[7] Researchers found that the diaphragm responded to different emotional states. Negative emotional states such as grief, sorrow and worry lead to a decrease in the activity of the diaphragm, with the breath becoming shorter, more irregular and in the accessory upper-chest muscles. Pleasurable emotions such as happiness and joy increase the diaphragm activity. Facial expressions also help. A smile and a happy breath are a powerful combination (we've all seen the 'have-a-nice-day' smile without the breath, it just doesn't convince us).

Rapport is diaphragmatic – the diaphragm responds in sympathy with others. This is why, when someone is really listening, really present, their voice has a very natural, conversational music. When you really listen to someone, you breathe with them. This creates a powerful, emotional connection when you speak. Their voice is in synch with you because they are breathing with you. It is very different when someone is thinking about something else or talking to themselves. Then their voices take on a very different quality. They pull faces, signal what they think you want to see, but their voices aren't dancing with you. It's dead inside because they aren't with you. It's faked and draining. Don't be that person. Don't fake it. Be present. Listen fully with body, breath and heart as much as ears. Then you will speak with confidence because you will be calm and listening.

If you do one thing for your voice, relearn to breathe diaphragmatically when you speak (it's something that we know as young children and then unlearn). I want you to relearn it. It will transform your voice and confidence when you speak. The final exercise in this section on the hitter of your breath will help you find its full power. You will then be able to take that feeling into speaking.

Try This: Weight Your Diaphragm

This was the big one for me. Truly life-changing. Do give it a go. It's also brilliant if you find it hard to relax at night.

I'd been struggling to understand and locate my diaphragm, but people who practise Pilates, yoga and martial arts understand diaphragmatic breathing and we can learn from them (see pages 140, 141). I was helped by a yoga teacher. Brian spotted that I was over-breathing into the chest and shoulders, he said 'Lie down there' and he put a gym weight on my diaphragm. It was in that moment that I got it. It's a very common practice in yoga to weight your diaphragm because the feeling of the breath lifting the weight up into gravity on the in-breath gives you a feeling of the diaphragm. Once you have that feeling you can find it anywhere.

For this exercise you will need two books – one for your head to keep your spine aligned when you are lying down, one (heavyish one) for your tummy so you can feel the diaphragm moving up and down.

It's entirely normal to feel sleepy at first when you do this. Your system is more used to chest breathing when you're awake and breathing diaphragmatically when you're asleep. Practise more, make this breathing a new normal, and you will find that you stay wide awake when you do it.

1. Take a book and place it under your head when you lie down. You can either bend your knees, keeping your feet on the floor – feet hip-width apart, knees moving towards each other – or you can put your lower legs and feet up on a chair (this can feel very relaxing because it eases the pressure on your lower back).
2. Place the other heavyish book on your tummy.
3. Feel the weight of your head drop. Let it go.
4. Relax your eyes. Let them be heavy. You may wish to close them.

5. Let your bones hold you up, feel the muscles soften and 'drop' through the floor.

6. Lengthen your back, widen your shoulders and free your neck. Relax your eyes. There is a phrase we use: 'Soft eyes, open diaphragm'.

7. Breathe. Find the reflex breath that we have explored. Remember that the breath is a wave. When you let it happen and get out of the way your breath flows out easily. Then there is a pause while the body waits for the in-breath. The breath flows in. Then there is a pause while the body waits before it sends the breath out. The purpose of the book is to mark this movement. You feel the book lift as you breathe in. The book is still as the body pauses. You feel the book drop as you breathe out. The book is still as the body pauses. And repeat ... Once you get the feeling of this it really helps to start connecting your voice to the movement. Speak as the book drops to the spine – try saying the days of the week. Then pause and let the book lift on the in-breath before you speak again.

You can also explore the diaphragmatic breathing sitting up. Place a hand on your stomach to feel the movement of the breath. If you allow your back to rest on the back of a chair you can feel your back ribs open and push into the back of the chair as the breath comes in. Practise this regularly and you will start to find you can draw on the power of the diaphragm to support you whenever you open your mouth to speak. The full, relaxed power of your voice will start to reveal itself, and your confidence will blossom too.

The Resonator: Your Body

An instrument needs more than a string and a hitter. It also needs something to resonate it. Though the larynx vibrates the air, the voice depends on much more than pure vibration. Your skull and the rest of your skeleton are fortunately equipped with lots of bony cavities that are excellent at resonating the notes you create. The note all starts on the string of the vocal folds, then the original note is resonated in the air-filled spaces in the head. This space in the throat, or pharynx as it's called, is like the body of a guitar except you can change its shape (try yawning and speaking) and thus change the sound.

And it's not just about the throat either. Although most of the resonance happens above the larynx, the rest of the body helps too. We feel something called sympathetic resonance – lower notes are vibrated as chest voice and higher notes are vibrated as head voice (see page 50). This resonance gives you *buzz*. Think of any voice that you love to listen to and I guarantee that it has an easy, attractive buzz in the body. It's as if someone speaks with their whole body. Your voice quality is partly nature – the shape of the resonators (your larynx, pharynx and soft palate), and partly nurture – specific habits you've learned from family and the world around you. But voices are more flexible than fixed as there are so many moving parts.

When you find an easy, embodied resonance in your vocal sound people will listen to you when you speak. There have been numerous studies over the years about voice in electability and they all find that we tend to vote for voices that have a low, centred quality, which explains why Margaret Thatcher was so keen to work on her voice, along with politicians since time immemorial. But while the world obsesses about deep voices, and people force their sound down to give them fake credibility, actually the voices we really want to listen to are open voices, not pushed-down, low voices. Don't force your voice into lower tones, it's much better to open up the resonance, to create more buzz and ease, because the whole body is relaxed and the sound is open. So how do you do that, how do you get buzz?

Try This: Buzz Your Sound – Open Up Your Resonance

Two things naturally open your resonators – a yawn and a laugh. Both are good to help you open up your voice. Space is good for sound, both inside and outside the body as long as there are hard surfaces to bounce sound back. Just think about how we sound better in a big bathroom than a tiny lift. Let's give it a go:

1. Feel space between your back teeth and keep that space when you speak, opening your mouth more than normal. Instantly you will have more resonance, simply because you have created the space.

2. To open your sound even more try a big yawn or a laugh. Feel the space in your head – between the teeth and in the throat – widen. Then feel that if you do a big belly laugh or yawn the body widens too. Notice that when you say something with a yawn or the feeling of a yawn the sound has an easy resonance. You might feel a lift at the back of the mouth, your soft palate. This creates a space in the throat for the sound to resonate.

3. Now say something with the feeling of a yawn and feel how the sound is open, rounder.

4. Place your fingers gently either side of your windpipe just above the collar bones. Keep them there as you laugh or yawn. Notice the windpipe widens, as you do this.

5. Now keep that width and speak – notice your voice sounds open. Remember to think about how the openness of a laugh or yawn can open up your voice whenever you feel tense. Come back to it when you have a quiet moment or before you need to speak with confidence.

THE POWER OF A YAWN

Yawning is a brilliant way to open up the voice to give you a lovely natural sense of space in the throat. You can do this before you have to speak, whether at work, before a social gathering or just before you start the day. If you do a big stretch with your whole body at the same time it's incredibly good for opening up the body, feel the space you create. Now speak into that space you've made.

ACCENTS AND RESONANCE

Different accents have different resonance, they buzz in different places. A good way to explore resonance is to play with accents. Try to copy different accents when you hear them on TV or radio: you will be reshaping your resonators to find the accent.

Try a London, Liverpool or New York accent and notice

the sound comes down the nose as the soft palate lowers. You can feel most of the air coming down the nose.

If you want to try the opposite feeling with the soft palate lifted, say 'aaaa' and feel the soft palate at the roof of your mouth lift up. Then say 'How now brown cow' and feel that very open space at the back of the throat. You will find yourself using a very old-school British received pronunciation with its round sounds and open resonance.

Sound-engineer Your Voice

When you are aware of how your voice buzzes in the body you can enjoy being your own sound engineer. You have different areas of your voice and you can consciously place sound there when you become aware of them. There's *head voice*, the notes that resonate higher up in the head. This is where sopranos typically sing. There's *heart voice*, where the sound resonates in the chest. That's where the altos live. And there's also *gut voice*, where the sound is low and bassy. If you can move your voice between these spaces as a speaker, you can become the sound engineer of your own voice with a fine degree of control because you can feel what is happening. You can add more of a gut resonance if you need more authority in a room, or find a warm, buzzy heart voice if you want your audience to feel connected. You can up the nasality if you want to project in a room, or you can remove it if you don't like the nasal sound in your voice.

1. First do a 'maaa' sound on a comfortable note and yawn it out of the body. We are now going to play with tapping the sound out of different parts of the body with your hand. You can do this sitting or standing.

2. **Gut voice:** Tap your tummy and back as you say 'maaaa'. Feel the sound buzzing low down in the body. Tap your back and side ribs and feel the sound buzzing in the bones of the body. Twist gently to shake the sound out of the body. Feel how it roots down low in the body, it has a connected, soulful quality. This is a great place to resonate from when you need power.

3. **Chest/heart voice:** Tap your chest Tarzan-style as you say 'maaaa'. Can you feel the sound buzzing in the bones of the chest? Think of someone you love and smile and say 'maaa' again as you tap. Feel the warmth of the sound in the chest. This is a great place to resonate from when you need warmth in your speech.

4. **Head voice:** Some voices are heady. Do a very bright smile and say a 'meeeeee' sound or a 'meeeeyy' sound. Keep the wide grin and tap your sinuses and skull. Can you feel these bright sounds buzzing around your skull? This is your feeling of head resonance. This is a great place to resonate from when you need energy.

You can up the headiness of the sound with nasality or nasal resonance. If you say 'nja nja nja nja', as kids do in the playground, you can feel the sound resonating on the nose and sinuses. If you cup your hands over your nose as you speak you can gently feel the buzz of your voice moving forward as you say 'nja nja nja nja'. This forward placement can be good for projection in bigger spaces as it travels well across a room. To take some of the nasality away, think of lifting the roof of your mouth (like saying 'ahhh' at the doctor's).

Articulation: Shape Your Sound

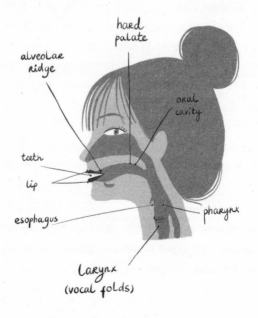

So, you are starting to feel in control when you speak, because you know how your instrument works. But there's a final aspect of your instrument that we need to think about: your articulation, the muscles that shape the sound.

The lips and tongue are your primary articulators, which are assisted by a relaxed jaw and energised facial muscles. The articulators give your sound shape and bite. They give you muscle. This muscularity makes you sound clear-thinking and articulate. It helps you to speak so that others want to listen. It also helps you connect to every word. Clear speech matters because it reflects clear thought. It also shows you care about expressing your thinking with clarity. It's not about accent – you can be articulate or inarticulate in any accent; what we want is muscularity – the speech muscles shaping the sound clearly. It gives you energy and commitment and has a big effect on the attention of your audience.

Improve Your Clarity

The best way to improve your clarity of speech, if you want to get a little deeper into the muscle, is to gently warm up your face, jaw, lips and tongue. Singers and actors often do a version of this exercise before a performance. You can do this at home in the morning to wake everything up.

1. Slide the heels of your hands down the jaw bones on both sides of your face and feel your jaw release. Let your jaw hang down heavy and feel space between

your back teeth. The more your jaw is relaxed the better you speak – it creates space for sound.

2. Now massage your lips and cheeks too. Move your mouth around, blow through your lips like a horse, then chew a big piece of imaginary gum, feel the facial muscles move. They are key to sending sound out. Say 'ooo' and feel your cheeks narrow to push sound out, say 'iii' and feel them widen.

3. Stick your tongue out – feel it stretch. Write your name with the tongue tip.

4. Say 'ma ma ma pa pa pa ba ba ba'. The lips shape the consonants and you want them working.

5. Say 'la la la' with the tip of your tongue. Feel your tongue move up to the roof of your mouth. Then say 'ta ta ta' then 'da da da'. Feel your tongue tip just behind your teeth.

6. Feel the back of your tongue by saying 'ka ka ka ga ga ga'.

7. Then speak; really shape the words fully as if you're speaking to someone hard of hearing.

8. Take that back to normal speech with a little extra edge of muscularity.

Clarity and muscularity make you feel confident and create a dynamic energy so that when you speak, the audience listens. It's crucial to learn to make every word work for you as it gives you real ownership of your voice. You say it like you mean it.

Be Bold

Voice is the expression of your aliveness. But sometimes expressing that aliveness can make you feel vulnerable. Remember though that the voice responds to practice. A step out of your comfort zone may need a little boldness at first but when you take that step you will find your voice and your confidence respond quickly. I put this to the test recently by joining a choir.

For a long time – even when I was training as a voice teacher – I thought singing was for other people. 'Good singers' auditioned for choirs; they had a licence, 'permission' to sing. But, one day, I heard a local choir singing. They were so full of joy and not at all precious about it; they were simply enjoying singing together and making a really wholehearted sound. As they sang, it made me a little bit tearful. It gave me a buzz to think about singing each week. I realised I needed a bit more soul, a bit more music in my life. I'd been waiting for someone to give me permission to be 'a singer', at school and beyond. But at that moment, I woke up to the fact that I might wait for all eternity. I had to give myself permission to be a singer, without needing to be a perfect one. I had a voice there, if I could just get past the anxiety. Sound familiar?

Fortunately, I didn't have to audition to join the choir, the only criteria were being able to hold a tune and give it some welly. I signed up before the anxiety had a chance to hit. Before the first session, my brain was full of negative thoughts. I was a bag of nerves. It was too risky. I might be criticised, judged even. I might look foolish. Or, worse still, be rejected. I wasn't a singer but I gave myself permission to have a go. To avoid panicking, I needed to coach myself through all the voice basics, which I am sharing with you in this book. I had to prepare myself before I went along.

The choir was more down-to-earth, more fun than I'd expected. We sang the Killers, Fleetwood Mac, Mumford & Sons. I noticed that when I stopped worrying I had fun. I went home with my whole system buzzing and resonant with the sounds of 'All These Things That I've Done' by the Killers. It really did feel like some soul had been brought back into my life. I woke up the next day with the music buzzing through my brain. I was proof that singing is good for you.

Am I a singer now? Yes, I'm a singer and I'm learning how to sing. And am I good, better, worse than anyone else? It doesn't really matter. I occasionally get a little paranoid that I'm the worst at sight-reading/unable to hit certain notes/wobbly at the top of my range, but it's not a choir where any of that massively matters. When you let go of the worry, you realise that actually it's about all the voices together. No one is worried how you sound. What matters is the harmonies that we make when our different voices combine – altos, sopranos, tenors, basses, all bringing their own quality. Together, we create something new. As individuals, we are okay. As a choir, we are *great*.

You are a speaker and you are learning how to speak. Have the courage to take the first steps to finding your voice, knowing that the more you use it, the more confident you will become.

Try This: Sing
(in the Shower, or Car, or Kitchen!)

If you want to grow your voice and confidence in just a few minutes a day, it's simple. Sing. Voice is good for you. Research has shown that singing can stimulate endorphin release, relieve stress and boost the immune system.[8] It's also a really simple way to get your voice powered up. When we sing, our voices naturally express ourselves fully. I'd like you to let go of any worries or shyness and be childlike. I've suggested singing 'Happy Birthday' in this exercise because we all know it, but you may prefer to choose a song you love. You may like to put the song on so you can sing along to it. If singing feels a bridge too far, that's okay. Why not start with humming along?

1. Sing 'Happy Birthday'. Feel how you take in the air before you sing. The ribcage opens and the diaphragm descends. You then let the air out slowly as you sing. Notice how you have different notes in the voice quite naturally.

2. Notice that there's a moment where the breath comes in low and wide:

   1. Happy birthday to you
   2. *breath*
   3. Happy birthday to you
   4. *breath*
   5. Happy birthday dear [name]
   6. *breath*
   7. Happy birthday to you

3. To bridge from singing into speaking say the words you have just sung or hummed. Feel the easy power

that your voice has when you speak. Notice how your energy has lifted, and with it your voice.

You will have noticed that your voice changed after you had sung. Think of the energy of singing and bring that energy (but not the tune!) to your speech. The next time you need to speak with confidence, sing early on in the day – or just before if you have space and privacy – and notice how your voice sounds more resonant and more confident. The more you enjoy using your incredible instrument the more confident you will sound, and it's an easy, natural, unforced confidence that comes from feeling good in your skin and sound.

Your Questions

Q: Why do I lose my voice?

A: The vocal folds are an incredibly delicate instrument. If you push the voice too hard on the folds, rather than using the power of the breath lower down, then it's as if you are clapping your hands hard for a long time and nodules start to develop. These are lumps on the vocal folds that interfere with the ability of your voice to vibrate. If your voice is hoarse or breathy and you can't hit notes you'd normally be able to hit, or if your voice is sore after extended use (rather than as a result of being unwell) then it's worth talking to a doctor.

Anyone can develop problems with their vocal cords, it's not just people in performance jobs and those who use their voices professionally, such as teachers and lecturers, etc. But you can learn to use your voice in a way that doesn't hurt the vocal folds. A trained speech and language therapist is a good person to work with. If you are worried about your voice do seek out professional support.

When we let the larynx relax and do its job, and leave the powerhouse work to the breath support lower down, then your voice will feel healthier and more powerful.

Three good habits to protect your voice:

1. Stand well (see posture exercises on pages 115-141).
2. Relax the throat and jaw (see resonator exercises on pages 48-49).
3. Find the power lower down (see pages 39-40).

Q: Why do I trip over my words?

A: The speech muscles require conscious awareness to get them to work for you. If you notice you trip over your words, or people have to ask you to repeat yourself, it will be really worth consciously doing the articulation exercises in the morning (see pages 53-54). Even a minute will warm the speech muscles up and you will find that they shape the words more clearly and you feel more confident.

Q: How do I get a deeper voice?

A: If you want your voice to have depth and richness, focus on opening up the ability of the body to resonate the lower sounds. The most effective way to find this ease in a way that is very natural to you is to breathe diaphragmatically and take the effort off the throat. Do the exercises for diaphragmatic breath (see pages 39–40) and also the posture exercises (see pages 115–141). Then the Power of a Yawn and Sound-engineer Your Voice exercises will help you open up your sound to access those lovely bassy notes in a way that is you.

Q: How do I get a more engaging voice?

A: When our voices are flat it's often because we've become physically flat too. Stretch if you can, take a walk for a minute or two, go up and down the stairs. Wake up your face and gestures and the energy will come back. If your voice is flat on a daily basis, there is really nothing better than singing: in the car, in the kitchen, wherever you can. It will open up your voice and energy so quickly.

Q: Why does my voice sound different on recordings?

A: If you hate your voice on recordings, you are not alone. There's even a name for it – *voice confrontation*. It happens because there's a mismatch between the voice we hear in our own ears and the voice we hear recorded. While we hear the note of our voices accurately as vibrating sound waves hit our ear drum from outside, we also get the sound inside our heads. It's this vibration inside your skull that gives you a sense of bass that others may not hear. When we hear our voice on a recording, there's also a sense that our voice is revealing us. It can make us feel vulnerable. A study in the

1960s found that when people listened to their recorded voices they responded emotionally to it because it both sounded different to how they'd expected, but also because it revealed how they were feeling, and what they were thinking in ways that they hadn't anticipated.[9] When you become aware of how the voice works, the more control you have over it. And the more control you have over it, the more comfortable you feel when you hear it – because you know if there's something you don't like you can make adjustments as the sound engineer of your speech.

SUMMARY: VOICE NOTES

- The first level on Maslow's hierarchy of needs is awareness of physiology. I hope you now have a good sense of how your incredible instrument works.
- Keep in mind the metaphor of your voice as a guitar: your vocal folds are the strings, your breath is the hitter and your body is the resonator. Learn to power up the breath, open the resonators and build the muscle of the articulators and you will play your incredible instrument with confidence.
- You can strengthen your voice through practice. Like Demosthenes, you can overcome hurdles with belief and practice. Find the exercises that appeal and make a little time each day to try them out. If you do just one thing from this chapter, notice how you breathe your thoughts. Give space for the in-breath as the fuel and let it power out your sound when you speak.

- Singing can help you find your voice, and can be a lot of fun. Be curious as to what you can do to use your voice with others, whether you join a choir or an acting or speaking group. Speak up more for a cause that matters to you. Commit to your new curiosity and notice how when you 'give voice', your confidence grows.

CHAPTER TWO

Find Your Calm Centre

In scariness or anxiety, breathe a little and you'll feel
the excitement. Hold your breath a little and you'll get
scared again.

FRITZ PERLS, PSYCHIATRIST

H ave you wondered why when you are having a chat with
your friends your speech is effortless and unselfconscious,
yet the minute you are thrown into an uncomfortable
situation that ease in speech vanishes? When life ups the ante
it can have some very audible, very visible effects on your
speech. And these changes can feel totally beyond your control. Your throat tightens, your breathing becomes shallow,
your heart races. Your voice shakes, along with your hands
and sometimes your legs too. It's all so exposing.

So many people fear – or even avoid – speaking in the
spotlight because this lack of control makes them feel unsafe.
But what I want you to understand is that when your voice
goes rogue on you, it's not because you are a bad speaker. It's

not a permanent state of affairs. It's not an identity issue. It's simply your nervous system's very reasonable response to what it sees as a threat. When you understand why this stress response is happening and what you can do about it you start to have real control over your speaking. And that control is key to finding your confidence as a speaker.

Wouldn't it be lovely to know that you can feel confident and in control when you speak in the spotlight – whether that's a live audience, a camera or a microphone? Wouldn't it be such a relief to say goodbye to rushing, flushing, gabbling and tripping over your words when you get nervous? That's our focus in this chapter. I'm going to show you how to find your *calm centre*. It's the part of you that stays calm and relaxed underneath all the stress. This calm centre takes you to the next level on Maslow's hierarchy of needs – safety. And safety allows you to access the part of your nervous system which makes you feel you are among friends. This takes you to level three – connection and belonging. So finding your calm centre as a speaker is a powerful way to step up your confidence two levels on the hierarchy of needs; it brings both safety and connection.

When you find your calm centre others will notice. In a sea of speakers rushing their way through their words you will stand out. The speakers we rate in TED talks, podcasts and videos all speak with this calm, connection and ease. They sound like someone chatting to old friends in the pressure of the spotlight. That's the quality you will have as a speaker when you find your calm centre. Now you understand the instrument of your voice you can start to have a degree of mastery of your nervous system when you speak.

You can learn to steward your system to safety and confidence anywhere.

- Let's explore the vicious circle of the digital age when it comes to confidence. I want you to understand how your gadgets are affecting your nervous system and how that affects your voice.
- We will take a look at what happens when your nerves get the better of you when you are speaking in the spotlight. I want to introduce you in particular to the two sides of your nervous system – which we are going to call *friend* and *foe* – as they both have a role to play when you speak. We will look at how to steward your system back to calm so you can keep this confidence anywhere.
- You'll learn how to find the calm centre beneath all the rush and distraction so that you can come back to calm and confidence every time you speak. You'll discover the power of daily rituals and find out why doing nothing just before you speak is everything.

The Tension of Attention

Attention is a funny thing, isn't it? You can be bathed in it by friends, in a safe environment, and it feels lovely. Or you can walk out on stage and feel overwhelmed, threatened and out of control. The gear change between ease and shaky loss of control is often beneath our conscious awareness, but it doesn't have to be that way. And when you know how to find ease in front of an audience, you suddenly have time to think.

You have space. You can respond to the audience as your calm-centred, best self, rather than the shaky, anxious version of you who may have shown up in the past.

Language often has clues – and answers – if you dig. The word 'attention' comes from the Latin words *ad* (towards) and *tendere* (to stretch). It literally means to stretch towards. That's precisely it, isn't it? All of those audience eyes on stalks, stretching towards you. And there's another relevant word for us that comes from *tendere*. It's 'tension'. There is always a hold, a tension in feeling a roomful of people looking at you. You cannot help but be held by their gaze. The secret superpower of effective speakers is that while they know that *tension* is implicit in *attention*, they have learned to welcome it as a warm, comfortable, supportive hug, rather than seeing it as a death grip, a stranglehold of stares that they have to defend themselves against.

You might have experienced this death grip when speaking in the spotlight – suddenly being pinned down by the focus of a roomful of people – it's not much fun. Your body reacts as if in the grip of an attacker. You tense, your breath rises and you speak faster. Your voice is flat and defensive. As a result, your audience tenses and seems less engaged. This makes it worse. The death grip can create a vicious circle that convinces you that you are a bad speaker. It makes you find reasons not to speak. It stops you practising. It can keep you awake the night before, worrying about the visibility, the judgement, the fear.

This fear shows up in those loud, 'confident' speakers too. You know the ones, lots of volume, lots of energy and lots of tension. If you look and listen closely, you can sense the fear:

the hard, staccato edge to their voice, the overdone, effortful 'confidence', the eyes staring just that bit too much. If I see myself in that zone on video, I learn from it. It tells me that I didn't get properly centred before I started to speak. Your audience can always tell when you're in that zone, because they literally feel the stress and effort. But you can always avoid that grip of attention when you understand a little about your nervous system.

What people don't grasp when they are panicking is that being in the spotlight can actually feel *good*. Rather than tensing and bracing when it happens, you can open out, give it a metaphorical hug and welcome it as a feeling of power. This allows you to step up and speak up, to turn fear into energy, grace and even excitement. Once you master being calm in the spotlight, you will have a wonderful, invisible superpower that will make others say what a natural speaker you are.

When you find your calm, the discomfort of the rush, the overwhelming intensity will be replaced by a feeling of space, grace and safety, even in front of the biggest audiences. So rather than being a runaway train, you will be calm and conversational, as if you are chatting to old friends. I want you to find a confidence within you that you can come back to every time you speak, no matter what is happening around you.

If you'd like to make the feeling of being under attack in the spotlight a thing of the past, then what you need to understand is what happens to your nervous system in the spotlight, and particularly what effect your devices have on you.

Devices and their Effects on Your Nervous System

Our current relationship with our devices is a dark and twisty tale of chronic stress, the autonomic nervous system, and compromised breathing. But it could be so much better... We need to awaken to the physiology of technology and cultivate a new set of skills related to posture and breathing.

Linda Stone, writer, speaker and consultant[1]

Have you noticed generally how much faster we seem to speak now? Have you wondered why? Do you ever notice how some days you seem to be able to speak with calm confidence yet on others you seem to be a rushing, jittery speed-freak? When I hear a tale of speaking woe my first question is usually: 'What were you doing just before you spoke?' Through the answers to this question I find that phones are often involved when disaster strikes for speakers. Most people let their devices run their lives now, and those devices are having a big effect on our nervous systems, and because voice is breath, they have a similarly big effect on how we show up as speakers.

When your voice goes wobbly on you, it's a real giveaway that you are in the *foe* system – *fight or flight*. Adrenalin, cortisol and blood rush to the parts of the system that will help you fight, hide, run or freeze. These age-old panic systems are a great set of options for survival but not for speaking. The voice, as we've discovered, reflects these changes in the system almost immediately. So many people connect public speaking with the foe system. Even the thought of a lectern, a spotlight, a script can lead perfectly rational people into fight or flight. And what's making it worse is that our devices take us into fight or flight too. The combination of a daunting audience and digital habits that stress you out before you speak is a toxic combination that will kill your confidence off at the roots if you don't take control.

Have you noticed what happens to your breathing when you check your messages on your phone? Linda Stone, a former executive at Apple and Microsoft, started to notice a pattern. Everywhere around her she saw people staring at their phones and holding their breath. Researching it, she found that 80 per cent of people in her study held their breath or breathed shallowly when responding to a text or email.[2] Other studies back this up. Dr Erik Peper, of San Francisco State University, found that when texting, participants tightened their neck and shoulder muscles and breathed shallowly and rapidly.[3] And when you breathe shallowly, you start to trigger anxiety. Knowing what you now know about your instrument, you may be realising that this is likely to have a big impact on your confidence as a speaker.

The problem is that our habits are changing fast and we aren't fully catching up with the impact they have on our voices. Voice is so often under the conscious radar that we simply don't notice what our devices are doing to us. The biggest challenge for most people when it comes to speaking in the spotlight is how we steward our nervous system – the key to our calm and confidence. So often I see people prioritising being busy – usually on a device – over being present before they speak. When you give someone at work five minutes to themselves before a meeting these days, what do they do? Most people, feeling under pressure, pull out their phones and work through their to-do list. And in those moments they let an unfiltered stream of people into their consciousness all demanding attention now: a tax demand, their boss, their partner who wants them to pick something up, stressful news from work, apocalyptic news stories. And a dancing cat. It can – not surprisingly – have an effect on your calm. It also has a very big effect on how you speak.

One client of mine was all set up and ready for a big pitch when – against the advice of her colleagues – she checked her phone minutes before they went in, only to discover that they'd lost out on a recent deal. She felt a wave of stress hit. She couldn't think straight. Her shoulders tensed. Her heart was pumping. Fight or flight was running the show. Her speech changed instantly as a response to this stress. She walked into the pitch going at warp speed. When she spoke she was loud, speedy and disconnected. Her natural ease and presence had left the building. Her audience were unimpressed and her team lost the deal to another company. Checking a text before the meeting had proved a very bad move indeed.

All of the above observations about your phone and devices may seem as obvious to you as the fact that smoking is bad for your health. But, like smoking, we get hooked. In his book *Understanding Media* (1964), the late Canadian philosopher Marshall McLuhan was prophetic about our unhealthy addiction to gadgets. In a chapter called 'The Gadget Lover: Narcissus as Narcosis', McLuhan writes:

> With the arrival of electric technology, man extended, or set outside himself, a live model of the central nervous system itself. To the degree that this is so, it is a development that suggests a desperate and suicidal auto-amputation, as if the central nervous system could no longer depend on the physical organs to be protective buffers.[4]

Without awareness, we essentially let our devices run the show. When you outsource your phone as your main means of self-soothing, you've taken a gamble; you're no longer in control of your own nervous system.

When we are nervous, like before a big meeting, it is natural to seek out instant junk comfort, and one of the easiest ways to do this in the modern world is via our phones. And the response that our phones creates makes us more compulsive. We check our messages more, we become less aware, more addicted. We start to use our phones to distract us from our nerves, when in fact we'd be better switching off our phones, paying relaxed attention to our nerves and doing something about the stress. Stressed-out screen junkie doesn't have to be your new normal. I want to encourage you to start to notice how your phone is affecting you. The first step is to pay attention to how you breathe when you stare at your devices.

Try This: Are You Holding Your Breath?

If you suspect that your devices are having a negative impact on how you show up, and consequently how you speak, there's some good news. In her research Linda Stone found that not everyone held their breath or breathed shallowly when they stared at their phone. Those who had been trained to breathe diaphragmatically – dancers, musicians, athletes, military test pilots – didn't hold their breath in the same way when they checked their messages. With the tools to manage their breathing – and therefore their adrenalin – they were able to manage their nervous systems and stay calm.

Linda Stone recommends that in order to keep our bodies on an even keel, we all approach our devices with the attitude that she describes as 'conscious computing'. Use your devices consciously and turn them off when you need to find your calm and confidence. Next time you are on your phone and you notice that you feel tense, check in on your breathing. You might want to try a little conscious computing now by picking up your phone if it is near you.

- Pick up your phone. Scroll through a few messages. Are you holding your breath? Is your breath shallow? Is the breath moving in your upper chest and shoulders? Which is likely to trigger the fight-or-flight response. Or is it low and wide, like a pyramid? If it is, great, because this is how you want it to be.

- If your breath is high in your chest, put your phone down. Put one hand on your chest and one hand on your stomach. See if you can gently encourage the breath into the stomach and lower ribs (you can move your hands on to the lower ribs in your back if it helps).

Make this a habit. Notice your breathing whenever you stare at a screen. Awareness is the first step towards taking control of your system.

DIGITAL MINIMALISM

The next time you have five minutes before an important meeting or presentation, here's a thought: what if instead of filling it with busy-ness (checking email, to-do list, social media, voicemail, etc.) you stopped and did *nothing*? Although it looks like nothing on the outside, inside, your system is slowing down. What if you staged a mini intervention on yourself and asked yourself if all the busy-ness is counter-productive to you being calm, connected and truly centred in your meeting? It might make all the difference to your success in that meeting, mightn't it?

I also take a hard line on making and reading notes on devices when you are speaking to an audience and when you are in the audience. It is a strict DON'T! My heart sinks when someone reads a speech off a phone or iPad because I know they will rush and lack connection. When you are in connection with other human beings, that connection will be massively enhanced if you step away from your screens and give people your undivided attention. They will feel fully seen and heard, and you will listen properly.

Steward Your System – Friend or Foe?

We don't see things as they are, we see them as we are.

Anaïs Nin

I was working with someone recently and as her breath slowed down and her voice became more relaxed she said, 'The room feels different.' The people in the workshop around her seemed to change as she relaxed and read the room differently. They suddenly seemed less threatening and more friendly. She'd gone from one part of her autonomic nervous system (ANS, your brain's basic survival system, see page 79) to the other. She'd switched systems – from foe to friend. (These are my names for the two systems; the scientific terms are given and explained on pages 79–81.) It's important to say that the foe system can be a good thing – it mobilises you for action. But it's my experience with clients that public speaking, that well-known trigger for fear in humans, takes so many people into the foe zone.

Nora Ephron's famous line, 'Above all, be the heroine of your life, not the victim' is worth remembering when it comes to speaking to an audience. I notice with so many nervous speakers that they feel like a victim who is at the mercy of their audience and the situation. But waiting for you is a parallel speaking universe where you are in control of your system and you are the hero not the victim because you can make any moment in the spotlight be one of calm, centred control and where you feel safe and connected. It comes when you learn to *steward* your system from panic to calm.

Friend or foe? It's the age-old question asked at every gatehouse for thousands of years. Foes trigger mobilisation in your nervous system – *fight or flight*; friends allow the system to ramp down so it can *rest or digest*. In our lives the system is working in a homeostatic way, balancing itself moment by moment according to the information it receives. And of course we all need adrenalin in our lives: a little arousal is a good thing. But what we don't want is to be in full fight-or-flight mode when we speak. It's exhausting for you and stressful for your audience. If you want to speak with calm, centred confidence then you'll benefit from seeing your audience as old friends rather than foes.

Stewardship of your system starts with awareness. First you need to be able to notice which part of your ANS is in charge (we will explore these two systems on pages 81–85). Then you need to know, calmly and without drama, how to switch systems. We'll look at that too (see pages 85–86). You already know the difference between these two systems, foe and friend, even if you haven't consciously thought about it. Think about those wrong-side-of-the-bed days. Those are foe days where your nervous system is concerned. You might have had an argument or a stressful text message or email. Open-plan offices with lots of eyes watching you, noisy cities with rude drivers, hard city streets that jar our bodies when we walk on them, a stressful commute, rushing to meet others – these can all stress us out under our conscious radar and send us into hypervigilant defence mode. When your fight-or-flight filter is switched on you feel stressed and jumpy and primed to pick up information about threat. Faces that could be neutral on a good day, look angry to you. You react defensively where normally you might glide through life. You might be aware that your throat tightens up, your voice gets tense, flat, stuck in your throat. Your body pumps adrenalin round the system so you can run away. As a result your limbs might feel shaky, and so does your voice.

Fortunately, you also know there's a you who cruises through life, who can chat easily with friends, moves with ease in the world. Those right-side-of-the-bed days. These are friend days.

This table shows you the two branches of the nervous system so you are able to recognise them in yourself.

	FRIEND	FOE
Trigger	Your system perceives safety, friends and connection.	Your system perceives a threat – real or imagined. Your system focuses.
Your brain chemistry	Acetylcholine	Cortisol Adrenalin
Heart rate	Calm, steady heart rate.	Heart rate speeds up, pumping blood to your limbs.

	FRIEND	FOE
Perception of the room	You have good peripheral vision and a sense of connection.	You have tunnel vision and become aware of enemies or exits. You might freeze as a last resort when fight or flight has failed.
Perception of audience	Seem easy to communicate with. Friends, equals. A peer-to-peer, relaxed chat.	Seem threatening, a tough crowd.
How you feel afterwards	Energised.	Exhausted. Can't remember what you said.

Why Your Voice Shakes

Voice is the canary in the mine of the nervous system. The shakes, squeaks and tremors are a sign to the outside world of the nerves inside you. You notice nerves quickly in your own voice, and in the voices of others too. Nerves affect us all differently. Some people speak very quickly when they get nervous. This is the flight response: 'Run away!' says your nervous system, 'faster!!' Some people go very quiet: 'Hide! Shhh! Be quiet!' says your nervous system. Some are suddenly too loud: 'FIGHT!' says your nervous system. Some go totally blank and the words simply won't come. This is immobilisation; the last resort. It's what a mouse does when a cat catches it. It looks dead. It hasn't decided to do this at a conscious level, the system has simply shut down. All of these reactions are deeply unhelpful for your conference speech or your big meeting of course. It's no wonder that these responses make us feel like we are bad, unconfident speakers. But it doesn't need to be like this. Armed with your understanding of your instrument and a grasp of the friend and foe systems, you can begin to take control of these pesky stress responses when you speak.

Counterintuitively perhaps, be grateful for the voice shakes. The rushing. The shouting. The whispering. The going blank. These responses are there for a good reason. They're not happening because you are a bad speaker. They're happening because your system has come to the rescue. It is helping you survive a bad moment and doing the best it can. You have to help it see that your life is not under threat and help it reappraise the situation. You need to teach it that the audience are friends, not foes. And even if your audience are a little foe-like, staying calm is beneficial because when your system mobilises to punch, hide or run away it locks down the parts of your brain that will help you think and connect. Fight or flight leaves you with very limited options conversationally.

Your Nervous System

In simple terms, your *autonomic nervous system* (the ANS) is your brain's basic survival system. It regulates your body's level of arousal. If you need to fight or run away it ramps up. When you can relax, eat, sleep, it ramps down. This system has two branches to regulate arousal: the *sympathetic nervous system (SNS)* (what I have called the foe system) and the *parasympathetic nervous system (PNS)* (what I have termed the friend system).

The primary task of the SNS is to activate the fight–flight–freeze response. It uses brain chemicals such as adrenalin and cortisol to ready your system for action. All the time it's scanning your system to keep you in balance. You might think the name 'sympathetic nervous system' is a little counterintuitive for a system that makes your voice shake and causes you to forget your words when you speak. However, the name can be traced all the way back to Ancient Greece to the root of the word 'sympathy', in the sense of the meaning 'the connection between parts'.

The friend system or PNS uses the brain chemical acetyl-choline to look after digestion, healing, sleep. It allows you to ramp down the system, enabling you to relax and connect. When you know how to access this system as a speaker you will have that lovely quality of calm and conversational ease that is so compelling to audiences. In these moments your two systems are working together, and you handle with grace whatever comes your way.

The SNS and the PNS work in balance in response to what is happening around you. When your system stimulates the SNS, blood is pumped away from parts of the system not necessary for survival. You move faster, your hands shake, your voice shakes, you go blank. These reactions can work in genuine threat situations where you need to run away, but they're not so great for your big moment where you need to speak with confident ease.

I want you to understand these two sides of your nervous system better. Let's meet them in turn. I'm going to personalise them with a pinch of artistic licence because I want you to get to know them, respect what each of them does for you so you can steward them as a speaker, and therefore find your confidence when you speak.

Meet Your Friend System

You know your friend system (PNS) well in the moments where you feel totally at ease in the world. If it were a person it would be that kind, calm, confident friend who makes you feel that you can step up to big challenges with ease and confidence. Who allows you to be yourself, to find your own voice, because they accept you as you are. In the friend system you find your ease and enjoyment in front of an audience. You can make yourself feel safe, even under extreme pressure. You are able to find your calm, clear-thinking self, your best self, when it matters most. That is when we are able to find our voices. There's real power in being able to move your state from anxiety and rushing, to space and grace. When you master this something interesting will happen. People will start to say you are a natural speaker, conversational, so at ease.

When you use your friend voice you:

- Speak with warmth and energy.
- Have a relaxed control of your pace.
- Use relaxed and expansive gestures.
- Have a natural and conversational tone.
- Respond, rather than react, to what happens around you.
- Sound calm and you soothe others with your presence.
- Are present, moment by moment.

- Look and feel as if you are enjoying the experience.
- Put your audience at ease because you are calm, they don't need to worry for you and they will really be able to listen to what you say.
- Will remember positively what happened. You don't feel tired, just energised.

What I know is if you can talk confidently to friends and family you can also talk confidently to a big audience with the same ease. Imagine the rock star who walks out on stage at a huge stadium venue: they have learned to make themselves feel safe in that intense environment. They might do this by thinking of the audience as one person, they may even identify one person (a family member, a regular fan) to talk to. Or they might recognise that the audience have come to support them, that they want them to do well. You can decide to think like this before you walk out on to your stage.

How To Find The Friend System

Actors have some fast ways into the friend system:

1. Deliberately breathing a feeling of relief can be a quick way into calm when you need it. Actors are taught to identify and draw on the breathing you have when you feel a sense of relief – that low, wide, easy breath that opens up the torso. Tune into the last time you felt a sense of relief, perhaps after an interview, or at the end of a working day, and breathe it now.

2. Imagining the feeling of talking to old friends when you meet strangers or people who you are daunted by is a quick way into the friend system. Even saying things such as 'I'm excited to be here, it's great to work with you' can allow you to feel connected and in control.

3. To access connection and safety actors are taught to think, 'I'm beautiful, someone loves me, I have a secret.' It gives you a gleam in the eye and a feeling of love and belonging. If you respond a little cynically to those words, I'd say don't knock it till you've tried it!

Meet Your Foe System

If the foe system (SNS) were a person it would be that well-meaning but stressed-out relative who has your best interests at heart, but they undermine you. Foe will say: 'Well, you know you could be really good, but you may not have done enough practice, perhaps that's why your audience look bored? Perhaps you should speak a bit faster to get it over with?' The intent is caring but the tone is worried. As the adrenalin and cortisol spike and the chatter in your head gets louder it can go really wrong for you as a speaker. Foe starts to scream: 'Get out of there! You're embarrassing yourself!' And you speak faster and faster. When foe gets going in front of an audience you speed up, your voice flattens, you become a nervous wreck. You start to feel that you need to hide from or attack the audience, rather than connect with them.

If that's you in moments of stress you might notice that:

- Your voice/hands/legs shake.
- Your stomach muscles tense for action and your breathing rises into your chest.
- Your mouth goes dry/throat tenses/voice sticks in your throat.
- You have a sense of tunnel vision, with everything happening at speed. You can't really see your audience properly and it's a bit of a blurry rush.
- You sweat.
- You speak too loudly (or it sounds like it in your head).
- You speak too fast.
- You notice yourself reacting aggressively or defensively, rather than with a measured response.
- You 'um' a lot and because you are too pumped with adrenalin for a comfortable pause, you notice that you are using nervous tics and/or recurrent phrases to fill the silence.
- You flush or blush.
- Your mind goes blank.
- Afterwards, you have no idea what you said. You feel exhausted.

However, a note of caution. I absolutely do not want you to think that the foe system is to be avoided. It's crucial for keeping you safe and focused. Foe has your best interests at heart, even if firing you up to help you run away or punch your audience is perhaps not the best option for that presentation you have coming up. But the more you remember that foe has a truly positive intention – it wants to keep you safe – the better. The more we can appreciate how it keeps us safe, the more it calms us down.

You need nerves, they show you care. So let's value the well-meaning, anxious voice in your head. Foe keeps you focused, alert, alive. But let's also keep foe under control. The art is to keep the nerves harnessed. To turn the fear into excitement. To get the butterflies flying in formation.

Try This: Turn Fear into Excitement

The key to harnessing foe to help you step up when you speak, rather than feeling swamped, is to manage the intensity of the feelings. What if instead of fear feeling like an unpleasant level of energy, it could feel like your power? And what if you could use this power to give you energy?

Reappraise it: Foe gets out of control when you feel the adrenalin hit and you start to panic about it because you see it as fear. But in essence the feeling is one of arousal. And arousal can be good. What if you welcome the rush and the intensity of feeling as a sign that you care? What if you reframe the adrenalin as excitement or focus? Think 'I'm lucky to be here. This is exciting.'

Accept the feelings: When the feeling of the adrenalin comes, breathe down into the intense feelings. Embrace the feeling so you can feel strengthened by it. Fear can become excitement if you breathe low and wide (see page 35). Welcome it in and it will fuel you rather than swamp you.

Come to your senses: Coming back to your senses will make you feel calmer. Slowly turn your head to take in the space around you. Filter for good things. Notice something you like near you. Repeat, more slowly. Looking for things that make you feel safe and connected will switch on the rest-and-digest responses, rather than the threat responses, in your brain. Peripheral vision also helps create a feeling of safety, because we go into tunnel vison when we are in foe and the system is looking for enemies and exits.

Say thank you: If you want to calm foe down, try saying 'Thank you'. Notice how a little appreciation makes the foe system quieten. As foe goes quiet, feel your feet on the floor, air on your face, come back to the body and away from the brain. Instantly you will feel calmer and will speak with more confidence.

As you become conscious of the foe system you will start to notice when your voice shakes how quickly you can flip your system out of anxiety.

Talk to Old Friends

Now that you know the difference between the friend and foe systems, how do you make them work for you as a speaker?

It's actually fundamentally simple. The answer is in the difference between how we pause for breath when we chat to friends and how we tend to rush and gasp the breath in the foe system. We don't gasp for breath in conversations with our dearest friends. We breathe in a relaxed way – low and wide, diaphragmatic. We breathe in our own time, we don't rush, we don't run out of breath. If we master this breathing under pressure, the voice will fall into place.

When it comes to finding the friend system as a speaker, start by cutting out the gasp – the noisy chest breath you hear in nervous speakers. Gasping the breath in audibly via the chest and shoulders takes you straight to foe because it's what we do when we have to panic or run away. It's effortful and it stresses out your system instantly.

Though I want you to avoid the gasp when you speak, it's useful first to identify how it feels so you know what *not* to do. I want you to do this now: pull in a breath by lifting up your shoulders and chest and gasping it into your mouth. Notice it has an effect on how you feel – you might start to feel more stressed, your thoughts may be speedier. Why? The body knows this as panic breathing and starts to create panic thinking. This leads quickly into fast panic speaking.

RECORD HOW YOU SPEAK

If you're not sure whether you gasp, record yourself when you are speaking - on film or just use the voice recording function on your phone. Can you hear a gasp? If you film yourself, you will see your shoulders and chest move as you breathe in, as well as hearing the gasp.

Try This: Cut the Gasp

The simplest way to cut the gasp is to close your mouth when you pause for breath. It requires you to put a break between sentences, and gives you space to take the natural pause for breath that you have when chatting with friends. Give yourself a moment to take a lovely, expansive, all-the-time-in-the-world breath, rather than the rushed 'tinned breath' (as John Betjeman called it[5]) that we do when we feel tense. And the benefit for the audience is that they get time to pause and take in what you have said and you have time to notice how your words are landing.

Practise the exercise below daily so that's it in the muscle and you can call on it whenever needed.

1. Think of walking around a summer garden and letting the smell of roses arrive in your nostrils. Notice how you breathe in that lovely smell; wide, expansive and easy. It opens up your sinuses, your body and your breath without effort. That ease and expansiveness is what we want here. Close your mouth and silently, imperceptibly – no sniffing please – imagine smelling the roses. Feel the air arriving in its own time, there's no gasp to pull it in.

2. Now, so that we can connect this relaxed breath into voice, let's imagine giving someone you care about a compliment. As you think of the compliment, imagine taking in the relaxed smelling-a-rose breath. It can come in through just the nose, or the nose and mouth.

3. Then say the compliment on the out-breath. Your voice will have a relaxed quality. How you breathe is how you speak. Just as a tense breath leads to tense voice, you are discovering that a relaxed breath leads to relaxed voice. You may notice that after this exercise your voice feels looser, freer, more relaxed. It's the voice you have when you are with people who make you feel safe. This ease is where your confidence resides.

I want you to practise this everywhere you go. Notice how you can pause – and imperceptibly smell a rose – every time you speak. If you can hear a gasped in-breath or a sniff, consciously close your mouth and take in that feeling of relief each time you pause. Notice that the breath comes in silently and makes you feel calm, whereas the gasp makes you feel tense. Try again until the in-breath is silent and relaxed, just as it is when you chat to friends.

Your New Normal

Realise the value of silence and [do] not be afraid of it. There needs to be space between words for it gives us time to receive and think and perceive. It makes us aware of our own inner quiet from which we can receive our strength and draws people to you. To listen well and recognise the need for silence, requires us to be relaxed within ourselves.

Cicely Berry, *Your Voice and How to Use it Successfully* (1990)

Now you know the difference between the foe and friend systems, the question is how can you make the calm you find in the friend system a default setting? Wouldn't it be good if there were a way to keep your system feeling safe and centred? If this could be your new normal?

The answer is found largely in the stillness and calm you can find before you speak. Performers are trained to take time before their moment in the spotlight to go inside themselves, to calm the system to find safety. They know that what you do to quieten the nervous system before the moments that matter can transform how you show up vocally, how you read the room and how you respond to your audience. You always get there early and you always have quiet time before you speak. This was drummed into me in actor training and I have carried it with me in life. But it wasn't until I learned about the science of the vagus nerve that I worked out why this quiet time – and particularly quiet time where I switched off devices – made such a difference.[6]

The vagus nerve is the tenth and longest cranial nerve in the body. It extends from the brainstem to the abdomen. Its name means 'wanderer'. Your vagus nerve (or ventral vagal complex (VVC)) sends messages to the heart and lungs which slow down and increase the depth of your breathing. The vagus nerve also controls the muscles that constrict the throat and produce the voice. So you can see that it has a big impact on your speaking. When you have good vagal tone you feel safe and you make others feel safe. Your voice is softer, more melodic, easier on the ear. It soothes others around you. When you have poor vagal tone your voice flattens out and loses the variety that keeps an audience interested. It stresses others around you.

Your vagal tone is crucial because it affects your neuroception – which means how you read the world. Whether you feel safe and whether you *are* safe are not necessarily the same thing. The same situation can look very different depending on how you read it. An audience in a conference centre or at a job interview could look welcoming or threatening and that often has as much to do with their nervous systems as with yours. When the vagus nerve is compromised you are less likely to connect to people and to listen. Your system fires up responses in the foe system such as a dry mouth, butterflies, a shaky voice and fast pace to your speech. Simply put, looking after your vagal tone means that you experience the world in connection and with empathy. You are relaxed and at ease. When your vagal tone is compromised, you show up as nervous, uncomfortable, threatened, on edge.

Vagus Nerve

In the words of psychiatrist Dr Bessel van der Kolk: 'When the ventral vagal complex runs the show we smile when others smile at us, we nod our heads when we agree, and we listen when friends tell us of misfortunes.'[7] Vagal tone affects how we filter sound. When your vagal tone is poor, your system will pay attention (and respond to) very low or very high sounds. These are usually of the threatening kind – human or animal aggression, bangs, roars, screeches. If you are addressing an audience, you will tune out the normal human range of the voice where the engaged connection is and only react to rude tonality and aggressive questions. A perfectly agreeable audience may start to seem threatening. A disgruntled audience might seem overwhelming. Whereas, if you take the time to centre yourself you will take it all in your stride.

You know when someone has good vagal tone because their voice and face are open and responsive. They are engaged, they see you, they hear you, they respond to you moment by moment, their eyes and energy dance with you. Their voice is melodic and alive. They are relaxed and confident. It's not a fixed performance that they put on to signal what they are feeling. They have a plan but then they allow their responses to be spontaneous. In a nutshell, good vagal tone allows you to be a relaxed speaker.

You know when vagal tone is not there in speakers: they are with you in body but they aren't fully engaged, they signal that they are listening and seeing you, but really they are in their own world of tension. The person's face is fixed, stressed. Their voice is flat. Their eyes are tense, they have tunnel vision. You might see them breathing in the chest, shallow breathing (see pages 73–74). There's no flow of emotions or voice tone, it all feels locked down. They may react to what you say in a stressed way. Eye contact is harder, they may stare or look away.

It's pretty clear that good vagal tone is a desirable thing, but the trouble is no one is taught about it. As Dr van der Kolk makes clear:

> Sadly our educational systems . . . tend to bypass this emotional engagement system and focus instead on recruiting the cognitive capacities of the mind . . . The last things that should be cut from school schedules are chorus, physical

education, recess and anything else involving movement, play and joyful engagement.[8]

No one taught you at school that the sport, the singing and the movement was actually what you need to draw on when it comes to speaking with confidence. Schools mostly teach us to read and write and use our intellect, then we take that into our working lives and forget the rest of the system.

We all crave connection, it's essential for our survival. But our devices are tricking us by creating a fake connection that feeds our brains but not our bodies and voices. You can connect with a friend on social media, but it's junk food. When it comes to speaking with confidence it does not feed your system. Our devices fire up our fight-or-flight response so your phone is not helping your vagal tone if you sit staring at it, breath held, shoulders tense. (It will help you, however, if you put on some music, or a mindfulness practice, so I'm not totally against all devices.)

If you want to create a new normal of good vagal tone then you need to calm and centre yourself before you speak.

Improving Your Vagal Tone

If you want to explore what it feels like to have good vagal tone, the key is to work on lengthening your out-breath. Way back in 1921, a physician and pharmacologist called Otto Loewi discovered that when he stimulated the vagus nerve it released what he called *vagusstoff*, later identified as acetylcholine, the hormone of calm. This became the first neurotransmitter identified by scientists. By breathing out long and slow – extending your exhalation – you can generate your own *vagusstoff*, stimulating your vagus nerve to send calm through your system. It's great for helping you find your voice under pressure.

1. Sit or stand somewhere quiet. No one need know you are doing this as the breath can be silent and easy, so you can do it before a meeting, sitting in a car, even with colleagues next to you.
2. Breathe in for four through the nose.
3. Hold the breath gently, for up to seven counts.
4. Breathe out slowly, for eight, through the mouth. You can turn this out-breath into a hum or send it out silently – whichever is more comfortable and appropriate for your location.
5. Repeat for two minutes.

Buzzing Bee Breath

If you want to take vagal toning a little further, a recent study showed that the vibrations of chanting and humming stimulate the vagus nerve, as well as benefit circulation and breathing.[9] This is called a buzzing bee breath.

1. Place the heels of your hands either side of your jaw, by the ears and slide them down, helping the bottom jaw bone to drop and release. Do this a few times if it feels good.
2. Keep the space between the teeth that you find.
3. Take a breath in and on the out-breath make a 'zzzzzzzzzz' sound like a buzzing bee – extend this sound on the out-breath for as long as your breath easily supports it.
4. Repeat this sequence. Breathe in, buzzing bee out. Feel your voice and the buzz. Notice how you feel calmer, more centred. You may want to yawn as the relaxation response kicks in.

Take a Half – Unplug

'Almost everything will work again if you unplug it for a few minutes, including you,' said the writer Anne Lamott in her 2017 TED talk.[10] How often do you unplug before the moments that matter? If the answer is rarely or never, then you can learn a lesson from the theatrical world. Take a *half*. The half is the 35 minutes of focused energy before the show starts. There is a wonderful set of photos by the photographer Simon Annand showing actors in the half.[11] What you notice is that it looks like they are doing nothing – they are staring into space, standing still or lying on the floor. But a lot is going on internally. They are finding a calm within that will allow them to stay centred and confident. Sometimes, they are doing gentle breathing or voice and body exercises.

The half made such a difference to how I felt when I showed up before a talk that I got a little addicted to it. I realised if I got myself calm and centred before a meeting I would find that the whole experience was so much easier. I didn't need to overthink things. I was present, intuitive. I knew when to speak, when to zip it, when to listen. The half always seemed to put me on my A game.

The secret to the half is to diarise it (literally put it in your diary or schedule) and commit to it – a meeting with yourself. It needs to be something that nobody else can hijack or cut into. It is as important as the meeting/interview/presentation that follows it. If you do this one thing I guarantee that you will start to speak with more calm and confidence.

Try This: Suggested Exercises for the Half

You don't have to take a whole 35 minutes for your half, although if you can, why not? How long you take depends on assessing how much the event matters to you and how confident you feel. If you are making a big speech you might want to block out the morning before so you can work from home and take a full 30–35 minutes to focus and get centred. If it's a meeting you feel low-level stress about then block out 15 minutes. What if you only have 5 minutes? That's fine, any preparation will help. Once you get used to these exercises you will find you can do them effectively in a short time.

- Turn all your devices on to silent and put them away where you can't see them.
- Open up your gaze. (Stress narrows our gaze, see page 86.) Take a moment to turn your head and see all around you, so that you can reorientate your system.
- Let your jaw and tongue relax; breathe out a sigh of relief.
- Bring your attention to your outer senses. Feel the points of contact your body makes with the points of support. Feel the weight of the space around you. Feel the clothes on your skin. Feel the hair on your head. Feel your eyebrows on your forehead. Feel the air on your face.
- Now take an inner journey. Feel your inner body: your guts, blood vessels, heart, lungs. Feel the bones. Feel the touch of the breath. Where do you notice it? Nose? Mouth? Throat? Lungs? Chest? Belly? Put your hands where you can feel the breath moving on the surface. Hand on chest. Hand on ribs – front and back. Hand on belly.
- Don't do anything to change how your body feels; just pay gentle attention. Notice what your body does when you leave it be. As you place your attention in the body and breath, notice how the mind quietens.
- If you are on your own, speak (you can count to ten for example) or do a gentle hum on the out-breath. This helps you to mark the out-breath, calm the system and warm the voice.

- Once you are centred, focus on three things to set your intention:

  1. **Your purpose:** What do you want to achieve? What will success be for you here?

  2. **Your audience:** What will success be for them? Who are they, what do they need from you? How can you help? What do you want them to say about you after you have spoken?

  3. **Your energy:** What is the quality you want to take into the room? Energy? Calm? Warmth? Power? What do you want the audience to feel? What do you need to do to find that quality of energy? Take a moment to gather up that energy.

Your Questions

Q: How do I make eye contact if I'm nervous?

A: When you walk into a room and you are feeling nervous a really simple way to help yourself is to imagine the person you are meeting is an old friend. That should help you feel more of a sense of parity and help you breathe (see pages 102–103). Also remember you are there to contribute. And if eye contact still feels uncomfortable, look between the eyebrows.

Q: I speed up when talking; how do I slow down?

A: Use the Cut the Gasp exercise on page 88. Close your mouth and pause at the end of each line. It can help to practise with a friend. Get them to put their hands in the air when they want you to pause, it will allow you to slow down and understand the pace the audience want you to speak at.

Q: How do I stop my voice and hands shaking?

A: Your voice and hands shake because you are in fight-or-flight mode and adrenalin is flooding your nervous system. So the key is to get into your calm centre beforehand. Practise what you have to say in advance so it feels relaxed and natural - you will feel more confident in the room. Before speaking switch off devices, take a half (see page 96) and calm your breath (see pages 73-74). When you are in the room imagine talking to old friends. Give yourself full stops at the end of each sentence (see question above), to give yourself time to breathe.

Q: How do I stop myself panicking before I speak?

A: Adrenalin is really just arousal - the racing heart, the flushing. This can also be a good thing can't it? It can happen when we fall in love as much as when we make a speech. So when you feel the rush come remember to find your calm centre, but it's also worth remembering that a bit of a rush is a good thing. It can help you: recognise it as a feeling of excitement and fun, a feeling that means you care. Come back to the vagal tone breathing exercises to keep you in the friend system (see pages 94-96). And switch off your devices.

Q: I worried for weeks before my presentation. It stopped me sleeping. Any ideas how I can avoid that in the future?

A: Take control of your narrative. First, visualise success: be your own film director and see what success looks like to keep you positive. Make a movie in your head of it going well – what do you see, hear and feel in the dream movie? It may also help to draw on an inner photo album – memories of times in your life when you've done something you were worried about and it went well. Draw on those memories as a source of confidence that if you could overcome nerves then, you can overcome them now. Then work towards creating a talk that you will feel confident about delivering because it's in your sweet spot of expertise. Hone it until you are excited to share it with the audience. It takes a bit of work to create something you feel good about, but that feeling builds your confidence and those building blocks can give you strong foundations as a speaker, no matter what has happened in the past.

Q: How do I stop myself going red?

A: Going red seems to happen most when we feel judged, observed and self-conscious. I also hear of it most from introverts and I think, as an introvert, that it happens when we feel we are in the spotlight and want to hide. And while it may be hard to totally control there are a few things that can help manage it: take your half (see page 96); find your calm centre. If you feel yourself blushing, focus your senses out on something in the room. When we blush it's usually because we are worrying about what someone else is thinking, so take your mind away from that. Feel your feet on the ground. Get into your senses and out of your thoughts for a moment to give yourself a break.

Q: It's good to know how to be calm and centred before I speak. But how do I do it once I've got started and the nerves kick in?

A: The revelation for people who get nervous in front of an audience is that you only need think about one thought at a time. If you find yourself getting nervous during speaking, just take a moment to come back to your calm centre. Feel your feet on the floor, the air on your face. Come back to your senses and your breath. This brings you back to your calm centre and gives you the control back. This can be at the end of every sentence or at the end of each new topic or point you make. You can always get a glass of water or throw a question to the audience if you need a moment to do this.

Q: How do I stop myself going blank?

A: Going blank is a sign of fight or flight (see page 69). The more you rehearse, the less likely this is to happen as it gives you a back-up drive to support your memory if the worst happens. You should also take your half (see page 96) to focus and find your calm centre. If the worst happens, breathe low and wide, have a drink of water, or ask the audience a question to get you back on an even keel. Feel your feet on the floor, the air on your face and return to the last point you can remember.

Q: How do I find calm and confidence when I am with people I am daunted by?

A: Parity is a word to remember in these situations. Show respect by being prepared, on time (or early) and respecting your host's way of doing things. This shows that you are an equal and a professional and this can bring ease to both parties. Combined with the right level of professional formality and respect required for the situation, this can be very powerful. I would also suggest smiling! The simple act of finding the subtle smile in the eyes that you would give an old friend will relax you and should have a good effect on your nervous system too.

Q: What happens if I'm tired?

A: Your half (see page 65) isn't just about calm. If you need energy, adjust your preparation. It might lift your mood to listen to some upbeat, positive music that you love. Move, get the blood flowing. Sing, get the voice moving. Drink water, eat protein. Avoid too much coffee because it makes you wired and can ramp up your foe system.

Q: What should I do if I'm really dreading something?

A: Do the breathing exercise on pages 94–95 to stimulate your vagus nerve to send calm through your system. Visualise success rather than failure and project forward in your mind to the moment when it's done. Sometimes it can help to think of a treat you have waiting for you at the end of the day.

Q: What if I have a very aggressive meeting and have no time between it and the next one?

A: If you don't have time to do the half (see page 96), then do this one thing: consciously relax your face. Find a quiet spot and take time to move and relax your face muscles. If you are in a quiet place give your jaw a massage and have a yawn and a stretch, it will reset your nervous system.

SUMMARY: VOICE NOTES

- There's no such thing as a naturally confident speaker. There are only people who have learned how to find calm and safety under pressure by stewarding their system from 'foe' to 'friend'.

- To find your calm centre quickly you need to make your system feel safe. Taking time before you have to speak or perform can really help your body, mind and voice to do that.

- Your phone is your pocket saboteur because it can trigger breath-holding and thus feelings of fight or flight. Holding your breath can make speaking uncomfortable, so learn to do without your phone before important moments.

- We think of speaking as something that makes us nervous. But actually, when we know how to speak without gasping or rushing, and to enjoy the pauses, we can calm ourselves down as we speak.

- In 'foe', attention can feel threatening. In 'friend' it can become a good tension; the feeling of being held, supported by an audience. You can decide to treat an audience as friends who want to hear what you have to say.

CHAPTER THREE

Get Out of Your Head: How to Embody Confidence When You Speak

Stand up straight and realize who you are, that you tower over your circumstances . . . Stand up straight.

MAYA ANGELOU, *RAINBOW IN THE CLOUD*

Guts. Depth. Soul. Confident voices have body, just as good wines do. They have this confidence because the speaker has awareness and mastery of how their body speaks, unlike most people who are talking heads. Numerous recent studies have shown that depth in voice has the power to capture attention whether you are standing as a political candidate or speed-dating.[1]

Why? Because we respond to voices that communicate confidence. We are in level four of Maslow's hierarchy, the zone of esteem. Maslow identified esteem as 'respect, self-esteem, status, recognition, strength and freedom'. The body is key to finding esteem and confidence. A feeling of strength and groundedness in your posture gives you a sense of easy, relaxed confidence and vocal power that others are attracted to.

You will find this physical core of confidence and presence allows you to stand up for yourself, to create 'backbone' rather than 'wishbone'. Joan Halifax, an American Zen Buddhist priest and anthropologist, puts it well: 'All too often our so-called strength comes from fear, not love . . . Instead of having a strong back, many of us have a defended front shielding a weak spine . . . We walk around brittle and defensive, trying to conceal our lack of confidence.'[2]

In this chapter we will develop your awareness of your voice in your body when you speak and learn why *feeling* your voice (not hearing it) is a great foundation to help you speak with confidence and presence (and to help you like your voice more).

We'll also explore the effect of good posture on your voice and confidence, and learn why text neck is a massive impediment when you speak and how to find practical ways to overcome it. You will also discover how to move with centred purpose on stage and find quick ways to open up your voice and breath through movement.

Your Body Is Key to Your Confidence

The Welsh word '*hwyl*' gives us the blueprint to the power of embodied voice. *Hwyl* is defined as 'A healthy physical or mental condition, good form, one's right senses, wits; tune (of a musical instrument), zest, gusto, enthusiasm'.[3] It is such an embodied quality. *Hwyl*, like voice, is full of air power – it comes from the Welsh word '*hwylio*', meaning 'to sail', via the Old English word for a sail. *Hwyl* is described perfectly in *How Green Was My Valley* by Richard Llewellyn:

> And the crowd made little moves all the way from the top to the bottom, not in restlessness but to find room for arms to have ease, for feet to be firm, for chests to give good breaths ... for room to sing ... Now open the throat, higher with the chin, loud ... Shoulders back and heads up, so that some of the song might go through the roof and beyond to the sky.[4]

It says something poignant that in English we have only kept the idea of taking the wind *out* of someone's sails, rather than putting it *in*. Llewellyn sums this up in his description of the school choir in the same title: 'Ah sang the boys and girls, with mouths like button holes, no tone, no depth, no heart.'[5] The school has taught children to sit down and shut up rather than stand up and sing out. And though most schools these days don't crush the spirit in quite the same way, they do generally require us to sit down and write. It's up to you to find your own *hwyl* if your life is sedentary and silent. You can get the wind back in your sails and the *hwyl* back in your voice when you straighten the mast, when you stand well to let energy and breath move freely around your body.

The digital age makes it so easy to sit and write messages to people, even when they are only a desk away. But you must use your voice or you lose it. The more you can connect human to human, rather than screen to screen, the more you stand up and speak, the more you find your *hwyl*.

So how do you create that dynamic power? By making sure you have a strong spine so you breathe well. By moving with energy and direction. These principles are key to confidence when you speak, as the body informs the mind of levels of safety (see pages 65, 90–95) and are essential to help you find self-esteem in the spotlight. As a speaker I know well that if I add a confident embodied presence to the skills and techniques from Chapters One and Two I know that when I step out in front of an audience I will feel calm, confident and free to be expressive.

You Are Not a Talking Head

You know you have a body, of course, but how present are you to it when you speak? For most of us it's a challenge to keep our attention in our body when our head loves to distract us. I've learned over the years that when people have very flat, fast speech it's often because they are expending most of their energy being their own inner talent show judge. They are listening to their voice as they speak and awarding (low) marks for note, quality and content. As they find fault with everything and joy in nothing it imprisons their focus inside their mind and makes them neurotic, flat, dull and fast as speakers. It's the opposite of what we want, which is a relaxed, well-paced, confident speaker.

I had to relearn to live in my body when I arrived at the Central School of Speech and Drama. 'Get out of your head' my teachers told me. It puzzled me and annoyed me intensely until I got the power of it. If it annoys you at first, stick with it. Sometimes the niggles are a sign that your brain realises the body may get a look-in. The whole of my schooling prior to drama school had lodged me firmly in my head. I wasn't a sporty child and wasn't good at games. School taught me that bodies were for netball, where you ran around and stayed quiet. For the rest of the time you sat down and shut up. I remember loving music and movement as a small child, but that stopped as learning got serious. So I wasn't taught to appreciate or understand how my voice worked, why how I stood could make a difference to how I thought, how my breathing could calm me down, why my blood sugar mattered to my concentration. My brain was the thing. Occasionally I did take action to make my body smaller or fitter, controlling it to fit an outer expectation of thinness, but my appreciation of the whole system just wasn't there.

I didn't learn to live in my body until this intervention by my teachers at drama school some 20 years ago. Like my voice, my body was there, below the radar. I hadn't mapped the connections between mind, body and voice, and didn't understand that the position of my head affected how I was breathing, that my jaw tension was related to a tight right hip. When I work with clients, I find that most of them have not made the mind–body–voice connection either. But when you make the connections, when you understand the extent to which the body feeds the voice, you find the confident, powerful voice you were born with.

Current neuroscience has a word for this process of bringing attention into the body – *interoception*. It's your inner perception – your awareness of the inner body that keeps you alive. In an age where we live in our heads at work, where we are constantly swiping and clicking, neuroscience has been demonstrating for at least 30 years that confidence requires us to balance Descartes' maxim 'I think therefore I am', with an equal amount of 'I feel therefore I am'. Psychiatrist Dr Bessel van der Kolk says:

> One of the clearest lessons from neuroscience is that our sense of ourselves is anchored in a vital connection with our bodies. We do not truly know ourselves unless we can feel and interpret our physical sensations; we need to register and act on these sensations to navigate safely through life.[6]

Try This: Be in Your Body

The good news is that internal perception can be trained. We can consciously do it. The first step to getting out of your head is to divert your attention from it and into the body. You then become less of a talking head and start to take on the embodied presence that is so key to finding your voice. One thing that helps me is to imagine that you are putting your 'brain in your belly'. Or if you prefer to be more like the Chinese with their idea of heart-mind, you might choose to centre your awareness in your heart. All that matters is that your awareness is in your body rather than high up in the head. It will allow you to speak with more flow and freedom and ease.

1. Feel your feet – how do they feel right now?
2. Notice another part of your body – bring it into your awareness.
3. Do you notice the emotions flowing through you right now? Are you calm, on edge, happy, warm, cold?

How to Love Your Voice

So many people tell me they hate their voices. Or more precisely, that they don't like the *sound* of their voice. This tells me that they haven't yet connected fully to the voice in the body. My advice to them is to turn off the inner microphone in their head and take their attention into the inner body to feel their voice instead.

When I lived in my head, I didn't love my voice. It was a bit of an annoying stranger to me. But then some advice changed everything for me: 'Feel your voice, don't hear it.' This advice was given to me by voice coach and director Barbara Houseman, one of the best teachers on the planet (see page 215), when I studied with her. It allowed me to make friends with my voice. It worked because it took me out of my head and into my body. Interoception is also the way into learning to love, or at least like a little more, your voice. When you *feel* your voice your attention is in your body, where the air flow that produces the sound starts. When you hear your voice it's in your ears where the sound arrives on vibrating air. Feeling your voice takes you to the part of the body that creates the sound, so you have more control in producing it.

That's why the more you can feel your voice and the less you listen to it the more confident your speaking will become. Listening to your own voice is a route to anxiety and self-consciousness. If you are listening to yourself, you aren't listening to your audience. When we listen to ourselves, we lock our attention away in our heads, our ears. Because we only have limited attention we have less bandwidth to notice other people and as a result your voice will be flat and lacking in confidence. It's also a waste of time to try to listen to your own voice from within. We don't hear our voices accurately, simple as that. As vibrating sound waves hit our ear drum from outside, we also get the sound inside our heads. And it is this vibration inside your skull that gives you a sense of bass that others may not hear. You don't hear what others hear. So not only do you not get any accurate information from listening to your own voice, it also cuts you off from the rest of the world. Don't stay stuck in the echo chamber of your own head, judging your own sound. Get your attention out into the body, and from there get your attention out into the world. Feeling your voice rather than trying to hear it takes you into the body directly and gives you enough feedback to speak with power and confidence.

Try This: Feel Your Voice

Feeling your voice is fundamentally simple. Your voice is vibration. You may have tuned that vibration out of your awareness because your thoughts have been whirling around in your head. But when you feel your voice you bypass all of that self-consciousness. You bring yourself into the pure sensation of your voice in the present moment and so your voice releases and becomes more expressive, more conversational.

1. Tune into what you can hear when you speak, inside and out. Say something and hear it through your ears. Hear your voice as you speak. Become aware of what it's like to listen to your voice through your ears as sound, rather than feeling the buzz of it in your body.

2. Now focus on your body. Say your name and feel what buzzes when you speak. Focus on what you can feel – the buzz, the resonance of the sound. It can help to yawn to find it because it's the most relaxed sounds that we feel in the body first. Then speak. Can you feel the resonance? ('Bone conduction' is the proper term, the sound buzzing in the bones; it can help to put your hands on your collarbones and chest.) You may feel lower notes in the ribs too. Then when you speak let your attention settle down into the feeling of your voice rather than the sound. It's fine to put your hands on from outside to explore the buzz. Play with different notes. As you discovered when you explored pitch

on pages 29-30, when you make sound the higher notes resonate higher in the skull and you feel lower notes lower down in the chest, back, belly and even the legs. You can play with the glide in pitch as we did on page 30 if you want to explore it again.

3. If you want to find your most naturally buzzy note say 'uh-hmmm' as if you are agreeing with someone. Notice how comfortable the note of the 'hmmm' is. This note is usually where your optimum pitch is. It's often a very comfortable central note for your voice. Practise that 'uh-hmmm' a few times and feel the easy buzz it creates. Enjoy feeling that buzz. Notice where it is in the body. Now say your name on the same note. Start to pay attention to the feeling of your voice in that sound. Can you feel where the sound is in the body? Put a hand there. When you speak, feeling the anchor of the sound can be very comforting and grounding. Staying in the feeling of the sound, rather than assessing it by ear is a really good sensory foundation for speaking with confidence.

When you stop listening to (and criticising) your voice when you speak and start paying attention to the buzz of the voice in the body, your voice magically improves. Your focus shifts to the simple fact of what the body feels. You are no longer someone listening to the sound of your own voice (whether you love it or hate it). You are a resonant, physical presence.

When your voice sounds thinner than you thought when you hear it on a recording it's because though we can hear the note of our voices accurately, we don't get an accurate sense of the buzz/resonance.

When you are tuned in to how the voice feels in the body, you notice that your voice is part of you. You become comfortable to settle down into it in the body, rather than listen to it and judge it in your ears. When you are already settled into the feeling of your voice – rather than worried about some auditory perfection – you are already immersed in your body and emotions. And because the body is where the voice and emotion starts, you become more in control as a speaker.

So, feel your voice, don't hear it. You will notice it gives you a different kind of embodied confidence in your voice.

The Power of Posture

All too often these days we don't 'tower over our circumstances' (see Maya Angelou quote on page 105). We sit at desks, hunch over our phones and wonder why it feels as if our circumstances are towering over us. Life cramps us into small boxes and when the moment to take up our full space comes we wonder why our voices aren't as strong or as confident as we would like them to be. The digital revolution means everyone spends a lot of time in their heads and peering forward at the glowing device in their hands. You know your tech is distracting you, but have you thought about what it's doing to your voice?

'Stand up for yourself.' 'Pull yourself up to your full height.' 'Get some backbone.' The connection between how you carry yourself and confidence is there in phrases that we use every day. Posture is the deep core of your confidence when you speak, it gives you guts and boldness – backbone instead of wishbone. It allows you to find an inner core, an authenticity that sounds good and feels good. A strong back gives you backbone and guts so that when you want to stand up for yourself, you know how to draw upon your confidence and power.

The simplest way to find the depth and guts of your voice is to stand well. When you stand well your diaphragm and ribcage can support your lungs to breathe freely and your larynx sits in the right position. Your larynx is only held by ligaments and muscles and if your head and neck are out of alignment your larynx can't do its job properly and that's when your voice becomes flatter and thinner – losing its confidence as your body loses its alignment. When you look after your alignment what you tend to find is that your voice naturally has more power and strength.

Because we are so visual, we often live in the front body. Our eyes are situated at the front of the skull and because there is so much to look at they tend to lead us through space, front body first. Now try something – walk backwards keeping your head in line with your spine, eyes facing forward (make sure you do this in a safe space). When our eyes aren't leading us forward through the world the spine straightens up really quickly. Notice how this feels. And know that our voices work better when we live in our backs. Next time you hear a good speaker look at their posture. Do they stand tall, with a straight back? If you're in a meeting at work, perhaps sitting around a table, notice how voices can get lost if someone is looking down or has a slumped posture. When you stand up straight and carry yourself with confidence, looking up and out at the world rather than eyes down at your phone, you automatically move, breathe and voice better. Your mood lifts (see page 126) and others perceive you as more confident. It's a very practical magic.

Good voices depend on good alignment. When your posture is aligned and open you create space – like the body of a guitar – for your musical instrument to resonate its sound, as we discussed in Chapter One. When you bend, fold or crunch over you close the resonating space and cut off the possibility for good breath support to create volume. Voice coach Cicely Berry makes it very clear:

> If your back slumps badly, the ribs will not be free to move as they might . . . If you slump your shoulders forward, you will find you immediately have to pull your head back to compensate for balance . . . when you pull your head back your neck becomes tense and the potential space is restricted so you will get little resonance from the neck . . . So you see one curve in the spine inevitably leads to another to maintain balance.'[7]

Try This: Stand Up Straight

This exercise is an oldie but a goodie. It really shows you how straight (or not) your posture is and the effect posture has on your voice. You will need a book and it can help to have something to record your voice throughout the exercise too.

1. Stand normally and tilt your head down as if you are writing a text on your phone. Say the days of the week. Notice your voice.

2. Now stand with your feet hip-width (the width of the front of your hip bones) apart.

3. Take the book and put it on your head. Let your shoulders and arms hang loose and heavy.

4. Notice how you have to straighten up into gravity to keep the book balanced, particularly that the back of the neck, the upper spine and your deep core muscles have to lift as if someone is pulling you up by the scruff of the neck. To keep the book balanced your chin can't be lifted up, or tucked down; it has to stay in a neutral position. Now say the days of the week.

What most people notice is that when your spine is straight, your voice has an easy power. When your head is tilted down to look at your phone your voice gets choked up in the throat, because the channel for sound isn't clear.

5. Take the book off your head but keep this strong spine. Say the days of the week again. Notice that when you keep this strong, straight spine, your voice naturally has more power and confidence. Standing tall allows you to find your voice.

Going through life with a book on your head is not possible but once you find the lift and stretch in your body and how it works for your voice, take that feeling out into the world. As life compresses you, keep springing back up. It can be as simple as standing up and doing a big yawn and a stretch (if you're sitting somewhere public you can make it subtle – a suppressed yawn is a fantastic stretch too). Notice what happens to your energy when you yawn to open up the breathing spaces. Recognise how it feels when you stretch to open up the body. Energy flows. That is how you create *hwyl* (see page 106) – open up the body, stand tall. You have so much more control than you realise.

Core Confidence

When you placed the book on your head you will have noticed that your postural muscles had to work to support

you as you lifted and stretched. Your deep core muscles (those in your abdomen and lower back) kick in. This is the transversus 'corset' muscle and it is crucial for posture and voice. When the spine finds its natural balance, the ribs can move freely and the breath has a clear channel. This core is also key to your voice power, so keep that sense of strong back, strong core there for you in tandem. The more you find the natural lift of the body (think the easy posture of a toddler rather than army sergeant) the more your voice opens.

Front Foot Energy

This exercise will help you find your natural centred voice and once you have found it via the core postural muscles you will be able to keep coming back to it. The idea is to get the whole body engaged in speaking, rather than just the head. You draw on the postural muscles to support your air flow as it leaves the body, upping the energy and power of your voice.

1. First find your front foot. This is the foot you lead off on when you walk.
2. Press the big toe of your front foot into the floor. Say the days of the week. Feel how the core muscles engage as you get on the front foot and notice that your voice has power and energy.
3. Now take the pressure off the big toe and rock on to your heel. Say the days of the week again. Your voice will have less energy.
4. Press the big toe back into the floor again and feel the power of the voice kick in. (This exercise works just as well when you are sitting.)

Here are a couple more exercises to help you find more energy in your voice:

- Stand facing a wall and push against it with your hands. As you push, engage your core and say the days of the week. Notice that connecting to the muscles that allow you to push the wall helps you find the power of your voice. Your voice will feel like it comes more from the centre of your body than your head.

- If you have the strength and the back health for it, hold a weight, stool or chair above your head. Stand tall, feet grounded and hip-width apart. Feel the postural muscles really kick in to support you. Speak the days of the week as you hold the object above your head. When you speak, feel these same muscles powering your voice out from your gut.

STRONG BACK, STRONG VOICE

A 2009 study by Richard Petty, Pablo Briol and Benjamin Wagner at Ohio State University found that body posture impacts the self-evaluation of the certainty of ideas.[8] Upright posture makes people more confident in their thinking.

If you want a strong, confident voice, the answers are in the body. In moments where you need to be confident in your ideas, the moments where you speak up, my advice is that you should also find upright posture. You will be able to own your thinking and speak up for your ideas. When you put some backbone into it, literally, when you fully connect to the body, the voice opens up. It's why actors voicing characters in animated films always stand up and always gesture. Move and your voice changes. Sit up and the right muscles kick in. The voice opens up.

Tackle Text Neck

As your alignment is key to speaking with confidence it's my belief that the biggest obstacle to finding your voice today is *text neck*, or *forward head posture*.[9] Try a little experiment now. Take out your phone and scroll through your messages or social media. Notice that you lean into your phone. What happens to your breathing? Where has it gone to? Is it in your chest rather than your belly and diaphragm? Notice your posture. Speak. Where is your voice? In your throat? When you hunch, a bottleneck is created. Your voice gets trapped and forcing it to come out from your throat feels like very hard work.

text neck

Text neck is a new version of an old problem. It's been around since there were scrolls to write on and read from. If we are not careful, it will be the next stage in our physical evolution. Day after day, we peer forward at our messages and slowly the head tilt/the hunch becomes our new normal. Your vocal folds (see pages 28–30) are positioned behind the thyroid cartilage (your Adam's apple) so when you restrict their space you restrict their power to function.

Your head weighs about 5 kilograms/11 pounds. With each inch that the head tilts forward from its natural alignment, an extra 4.5 kilograms/10 pounds of load is added to the spine.[10] You have to start using muscles that shouldn't need to be used – the jaw, for example – just to hold you up. Tension in the neck and jaw can feed into tension in the voice. It may even have an effect on the resonance of your voice.[11] While you may understand that this posture isn't brilliant for your spine's health, what you may not realise is that it's also a big blocker to finding the expressiveness and emotional connection, not to mention the power, that is so key to finding your voice. One study found the forward head posture expanded the upper rib-cage, while contracting the lower ribcage.[12] If you look at a picture of the lungs (see page 36), you will realise that the lungs have most capacity lower down. If you cut off your lower tho-rax/ ribcage you lose lung capacity. What you will be realising is that because text neck reduces your breath capacity it also has an impact on your voice power.

It gets worse. Text neck can increase your anxiety levels too. When you're uncentred like this, with poor posture, your shoulders become tense. Your body closes down, your shoulders rounding. Leaning down into a phone – head down, eyes down, breath high in the chest – is a posture of defensiveness and your body reacts as if there is danger and that triggers your fight-or-flight stress responses (see pages 78–79). When you take that stress response and combine it with the pressure of a big audience it can spin your system into abject panic. If your body is in a posture of submission or defensiveness because you've been checking your messages, it is not surprising that when you speak you send out the wrong signals to an audience.

Because text neck is a postural habit that so many people have, it presents you with a golden opportunity to be different. If you stand up straight and tower over your circumstances – with a centred voice, relaxed breathing and aligned posture – you become one of the speakers that people want to listen to. Overcoming text neck is part self-discipline, part conscious awareness. Here are a couple of exercises for you to try.

Try This: Text Neck Check

Look at photos and videos of yourself. Is your head poking forward? If it is, you have text neck.

Another way to check is to sit or stand against a wall and check your phone. If it feels weird to keep your head against the wall as you check your phone then your habit is text neck.

Try This: Ears Over shoulders

As a quick way out of text neck, it often helps to remember that your body knows how to speak with confidence; you were built to be able to do it. Young children naturally have strong backs to balance those outsize heads on. As an adult, you naturally have to align yourself when you have to balance on a wobbly train or walk on a mountain path. Your strong back is still there, you just have to work on it!

You need to ask yourself: 'Are my ears over my shoulders?' Because they should be. If at any point in the day you realise that you have text neck and your head is peeping over your shoulders, remind yourself: 'Ears over shoulders'. I particularly try to notice it when I'm tired or if I've been on a device for too long. It's interesting how the hunch happens when we're feeling tired or low. If you can catch it and think 'Ears over shoulders' it helps your mood as much as your voice.

To do it:

1. Imagine someone pulling you up from the scruff of the neck, like when a puppy is picked up by its mum.
2. Now move the top of your head and the tips of your ears over your shoulders.
3. Notice how the back of your neck flows up easily out of your spine, with your head balanced on top not pushed forward off it. This is your natural spine alignment and is how your body is designed to be!

EFFECTIVE EXERCISE FOR TEXT NECK AND POSTURE

The Weight Your Diaphragm exercise on pages 43-46 is a great one to do each day. It comes from Alexander technique, which is discussed on pages 139-140.

Strength and Softness

What you will find when you look after your posture is that standing well gives you a new kind of strength combined with softness. It's a strength that is fluid and flexible because it's of the body and breath, rather than the fixed brittle sense of ourselves that comes from our conceptual thinking when we are stuck in our heads. The *strong back* of your embodied presence allows a *soft front* of connection. And this feeds into your voice.

A recent study explored how people responded to different voices saying 'Hello' and found that those with a mixture of trust, strength and likeability were the most highly rated. They found that listeners rated the utterances consistently and that trust and likeability (softness) combined with dominance (strength) were key features.[13]

Try This: Strong Back, Soft Front Meditation

This meditation, from the work of Joan Halifax, is a great way to come back to both your strength and softness.[14] It gently reminds you of the power of posture and its impact on your confidence. You can do this exercise whenever you want, but it might be particularly useful to do at home before a big day or right before you speak.

1. Bring your awareness into your spine. Breathe into it. Appreciate how strong and aligned it is.
2. Close your eyes and imagine the full length of your spine. Feel your body's flow of energy up and down the spine.
3. Rock gently, from side to side, as you settle your posture.
4. Notice your breathing. Think of the breath cycle: breathe in as air flows down your spine and breathe out as the air flows up your front, gently zipping up. Now let your awareness go to your belly. Breathe into your belly. Let your breath be deep and strong as your belly rises and falls.
5. The strength of your spine allows you to uphold yourself in the middle of any situation. You can remind yourself of this strength by silently saying 'Strong back'.
6. Your mind and your back are connected. Feel the sense of uprightness and flexibility in your mind.

7. Feel your natural courage and openness as you breathe deeply into your belly. Shifting your awareness to your chest, touch the tender, open feeling of this space.
8. Feel the strength of your resolve rising up from your belly. Let your heart be open and permeable.
9. Release any tightness as you allow your breath to pass through your heart. Remind yourself of your own tenderness by saying 'Soft front'.

Relaxed Body = Confident Speaker

Speaking in the modern world can be confusing. The desired conversational style requires that you are prepared, your content is polished but your delivery is relaxed. Relaxed but on point – good posture, committed, open expression, eyes up and voice clear. The art to this paradox is to find a way to be as you are, at your best. When we are feeling great we are grounded and physically present, we are expansive and we move with energy and direction. We don't try to hide away.

The key to speaking in front of an audience is to make it feel as if you are in your sitting room with old friends. So often people walk out in front of an audience and they look terrified and small. They make themselves look like a victim rather than a confident speaker. Using a Shakespeare play as an analogy, they have cast themselves as the terrified servant in the scene rather than the all-powerful queen or king. I'm not asking you to go full TV preacher or late-night chat show host, don't panic. But I do want you to find the natural confidence you have when you are at your best. Viv Groskop calls it 'happy high status' in her great book *How to Own the Room* (2018), which I love.

You can think about it on a scale of 1 to 10. Using the Shakespeare analogy again, level 1 is the servant and level 10 is the monarch. In your own life, when you are with friends you are at level 5 – easy, relaxed, on point. In a small meeting this is fine. But when the spotlight is on you, go up, find level 8.

I'm going to give you the tools to find that spotlight confidence over the next few pages, from the feet up, because that's where we want your confidence to start.

Feet on the Ground

'She's got her feet on the ground.' That familiar phrase tells you of easy confidence and trust in oneself. Getting your feet firmly planted on the ground is essential to finding your voice. To speak with confidence you will need to think about your feet and we are going to look at why, and how, you do this.

When you walk across a room towards a friend you are relaxed and simply focused on getting to that person. You aren't worrying about what they think of you. So if you want to speak with confidence you need to find the same easy presence to movement.

Research shows that even imagining walking on concrete pavements jars our bodies and changes our breathing and can thus trigger fight or flight. Whereas when imagining you are standing on soft ground in bare feet and you let your feet relax, it sends a message to your system to relax.[15] Laurence Olivier told actors to 'Relax your feet and always have more breath than you need'. Your feet need to feel relaxed and comfortable for your system to feel truly safe. Choose your shoes with care: anything that pinches, hurts or physically takes you off balance may cramp your style or take you off balance in a bigger sense. If you are preparing to speak, whether at a business event, a talk, or even a party, value your voice over your footwear! Choose shoes that help you *ground* your feet. High heels are tricky as they make some people feel more confident, but if you pay attention to your voice they tend to curve your lumbar spine, send the breath into the chest and make you sound nervous.

A good rule of thumb is if you can't comfortably walk in a pair of shoes (and teetering is not walking comfortably) they will affect your voice. Find shoes that you can move in naturally and that give you confidence with enough comfort to allow you to breathe and voice with ease.

Try This: Find Your Roots

This exercise teaches you to connect with the ground, in a literal way, helping you to feel grounded. If you can, when you try this exercise for the first time do it with your shoes off. Once you get the hang of it, it becomes something you can do anywhere: when you walk out on stage, into a meeting, etc. Keep the feeling of relaxation in your feet when you speak. If you notice that you have lost your sense of stillness and strength, come back to the feeling of your feet on the ground.

1. Stand with your feet hip-width apart. Feel your feet relax into the floor. Imagine breathing through the pores of your feet if this helps.
2. Relax your legs and drop your tail bone, feeling your lower back lengthening.
3. Imagine your favourite place in the natural world, whether a beach, a park, a garden. Imagine standing barefoot on the soft ground, feel your feet relax. Imagine that you have roots going through the soles of your feet, down into the earth below, spreading out to the front, back and sides of you.

Keep a sense of those roots when you are in front of an audience. Walk out on stage, plant roots and breathe. Move on a pause – don't talk and move at the same time as it distracts people. Find a new point on stage, plant roots, breathe and speak. This will make you feel safe in front of the biggest audiences.

What to Do with Your Hands

Many of my clients ask me what they should do with their hands when they are speaking. The simple answer is that when your body is centred, with good, relaxed posture, you will find that your hands move naturally. When you have that feeling of confidence and esteem then the skill is to draw on your repertoire of natural gestures.

If you think you need to work on what to do with your hands, there are a few things you can try and I find these work well with my clients:

Observe yourself in relaxed situations: Find your natural gestures – notice what you do when you are relaxed and at ease (you may find it helpful to video yourself) – at dinner, glass of wine in hand, chatting happily. Those are the gestures that will also help you express your ideas in front of an audience.

Observe your nervous tics: Notice what you do when you get nervous. Do you cross your arms? Grip your hands or a pen? Point? Put your hands behind your back? You need to stop these tics. It takes a little discipline to notice them when they show up but if you breathe and relax your shoulders then your hands will relax. If you are worried your nervous gestures will surface when you speak, do some rehearsals on video and see if you can cut them out. Or get a friend to watch you rehearse and call out each time you fall back into nervous habits. You can stop nervous twitches pretty quickly when you pay attention to them.

Relax your body: The absolute best way to ensure that you always know what to do with your hands is to relax your shoulders, hips and ribs. When performers warm up they shake out and swing their legs, arms and shoulders. They know that when the body is relaxed you don't have to worry about what to do with your hands as your body will be able to move more naturally.

Try This: Shoulder Rolls and Swings

This is great to do before you speak. Do it whenever and wherever works for you. I trust you to know which parts of this exercise are right for you to do (and to choose what works for the space you're in).

1. Pick up your shoulders on the in-breath, drop them on the out-breath.
2. Roll your shoulders slowly forward in a circle. Roll them back. Do this five times.
3. Checking you won't hit anything, swing your right arm forward and back. Do full circles if that feels good. When you've done ten circles, swap over to your left arm.
4. Give your hands a gentle shake out to release any tension.
5. Finally – and you can pay attention to this all day – keep your shoulders wide and open. It can help to imagine angel wings!

How to Expand Your Confidence on Stage

The pressure and visibility of the spotlight can make people want to close down, to cross their arms, to hide behind the lectern or focus on laptops and devices. We feel like we want to shrink, for the earth to swallow us up.

The secret to speaking with confidence is to feel the fear of the spotlight and consciously open up, not close down. As a speaker in front of an audience you need to take up more space than you would naturally in a one-to-one conversation. When you stand correctly and allow your gestures to be open and expressive, your voice and energy open up too.

Try This: The Magnificence

I was taught this exercise as 'The Magnificence', which is a great name because it does really make you feel a little bit more magnificent. You can apply everything we have done so far in this chapter to this exercise. Do this at home in the morning before your speaking engagement or in the space you are speaking in if no one is around.

1. Centre yourself in your body. Relax your feet. Hold yourself well – imagine that book on your head – and find your full height and your deep core strength, the source of your power.

2. Open your arms wide making sure you can see your fingertips on either side in your peripheral vision. As you speak the days of the week let your voice and energy flow out beyond your conversational space to fill the whole room.

3. Let your arms slowly drop but keep a sense of this peripheral vision and your increased personal space. Speak the days of the week filling this bigger space.

Energy and Direction

Once you have a core of confidence in the body and understand how to expand your personal sense of space when you are in the spotlight, the next step is to stay centred when you move.

Watch any confident speaker and you will see them move with unselfconscious ease and purpose in front of an audience. They have energy and direction.

You already know how to move with ease, energy and direction because you do it when you're relaxed. Think about a sunny holiday morning, you are comfortable in your skin, you move because you want to do something. The movement is simple and purposeful.

Now remember the last time you felt anxious when you walked out in front of an audience, or had to raise a hand or stand to speak. The gaze of the audience can make a simple act of walking, or standing, or raising a hand, things you do every day, seem strange, self-conscious and gawky. There's so much twitchy, self-conscious thinking going on in your head and it feeds into the body as nervous fidgeting.

Anxiety makes us hyper-alert to our inner world. We second guess what others are thinking, we catastrophise how badly we are going to mess up. We create a psychodrama/disaster movie that takes over our brains. It's the thinking that creates the twitching. And when we get fidgety and anxious it makes others worry about us – it's infectious.

The question is: if you know you can move with relaxed purpose in certain situations, how can you do it when walking out on a stage or into a meeting room full of people? The answer is simple: model what you already do well by breaking out of your anxious thinking. The technique you will need is called 'Camera Out'.

Try This: Camera Out

I most often teach this technique to people who like to live in their heads, analysing every move. They are often jerky and twitchy when anxiety hits, overthinking everything. If this is you, the simple antidote is to learn to be more in your senses – camera out – than your thinking. Speaking is physical so it is sensible to become aware of your senses as you move. Take the advice my teachers gave me and 'Get out of your head' (see page 108).

The key is to model what you do when you are relaxed. When you walk across a summer garden on holiday you set a direction and then you move with a clear straight arc of energy. (If you want to see a master of this direction in movement watch a great dancer or tennis player – the movement is clear and purposeful.) When you move like this your senses are engaged in taking you in that direction.

1. Come into your senses, camera out. What can you see, hear, feel, smell, taste that you haven't noticed before? This sharpens your camera out. It quietens your inner thinking.
2. Now choose a point you want to walk to. Set a direction and move towards it, keeping your attention on what you can see, hear, feel, smell, taste as you move.

Get to where you want to get to. Stop, breathe, ground your feet on the floor.

When I am working with a speaker I always help them practise moving with camera out, pausing with camera out. It allows you to look relaxed and conversational and means that when you move in the spotlight you do it with relaxed energy and direction. You will notice that when your movement is confident, your speech will be too.

Further Work on Your Posture

If you want to do further work on your posture then you can learn from athletes, dancers, singers and other performers (and lots of non-performers too – me included) and find a trained Alexander technique, yoga or Pilates teacher. These disciplines are all brilliant at helping you understand how to find the alignment and space in the body that will allow you to move and speak with confidence and ease.

Finding a teacher to work with you one-to-one is the best approach. There are great group classes and there is so much online now, but if you can I'd recommend having a few lessons in person with a trained teacher first as we are often blind to our habits and a teacher can easily point these out to you and give you things to work on.

Alexander Technique

Alexander technique is a powerful system to support you in finding your voice and I cannot recommend it highly enough. Its creator, Frederick Matthias Alexander, was born in 1869 in Tasmania. He became a reciter of dramatic pieces in his youth. But he began to lose his voice and doctors didn't seem to be able to help. Despairing, he started to observe himself in a mirror and realised that how he held himself when he was reciting, the postures that felt to him strong and confident, were actually causing his vocal problems. He taught himself to, as he put it, find a new 'use' for his musculature. His voice recovered. And as Nikolaas Tinbergen said of Alexander's work in his 1973 Nobel lecture: 'This story, of perceptiveness, of intelligence, and of persistence, shown by a man without medical training, is one of the true epics of medical research and practice'.[16]

Alexander wasn't a man to stop there. He could see that he wasn't alone in having habits that prevented finding natural ease and grace in both voice and movement. He began to teach his method to others and his students took on the work. Now Alexander technique is one of the staples of performance training. I came across it there, but one-to-one lessons have helped me sleep better, move with more grace and find a calm I never thought I would have. And it has helped my voice find its natural freedom. As Tinbergen also said in his Nobel lecture, he noticed 'with growing amazement, very striking improvements in such diverse things as high blood pressure, breathing, depth of sleep, overall cheerfulness and mental alertness, resilience against outside pressures, and also in such a refined skill as playing a stringed instrument.'[17]

So, what happens in an Alexander technique lesson? Teachers very gently notice your patterns of movement and then guide you to the best 'use' of your body to help you discover an alignment that allows for natural ease of movement. It's the unrestricted freedom of movement that we have as very small children. They take you back to basics: you learn to stand, walk, sit and lie down using the simple movements that are intuitive to the body beneath the accretions of habits that you may have developed. You find that as you access the natural freedom and grace of the spine you find relaxation and ease: it's a lovely feeling that starts to infuse your life with new calm.

My experience of Alexander technique has been similarly transformational to Tinbergen's. It has been the key to helping me find a new calm and centredness that feeds seamlessly into my life.

Pilates

Used widely in the dance world, and now increasingly popular in the mainstream, Pilates is a method designed by Joseph Pilates. It is used to open up the breath and body. Working with gravity to help the body find space for breath is a great way to explore how you can breathe, voice and move with more power and ease. Pilates exercises are simple enough, challenging enough and 'deep' enough to delve into for a lifetime. There are different kinds of Pilates. The purest form is classical Pilates which works with Joseph Pilates' exercises as he created them. You will use the equipment – the reformer, the chair, the cadillac, etc. – that he designed to help you understand the exercises more deeply because they provide extra weight to work into. It's incredibly helpful for mind, body and breath. There are many other good forms to explore and if classical Pilates is not available near you look for Pilates teachers with a dance background and a focus on opening up the breath through the movement as you build deep core support. Do find out about your teacher's training – you need to know that they have done proper training for at least a year and ideally have dance or performance training in the muscle prior to that.

Yoga

There are many yoga classes out there, for all levels of ability. If you are a beginner choose a beginners' class or a mixed-level class. Tell the teacher you are a beginner, and if you have any injuries. The teacher will take you through a series of asanas, or movements, that will open up your body and breath. The word yoga means yoke and its aim is to harness mind–body–breath.

There are lots of different kinds of yoga – hatha is often a good place to start as classes tend to cover the essentials. Ashtanga, dynamic and power yoga tend to be fast classes and if you are athletic you will get the hang of them quickly but they are not for everyone, certainly not at first. Iyengar yoga was extremely helpful for me because it teaches detailed posture which is key for the voice. Yin and restorative yoga are wonderful for deep stretching and relaxation – really great for voice and breath. You can also find classes where you learn to chant – this is a wonderful way to open up your voice if it appeals.

Your Questions

Q: My voice feels very flat when I've been at a desk all day. What can I do?

A: Here are three quick exercises that should liven up your voice.

1. Shake out – find a quiet space. Shake out your left hand and arm, right hand and arm, left leg and foot, right leg and foot (hold on to something if you need to balance).
2. Tap out – get the blood flowing. Using your hands, tap down the front of your left leg and up the back of the left leg; do the same with your other leg and with each arm. Gently tap, like raindrops, the top of your head with your fingers. Then if you can make sound, tap your chest and say 'maaa'. Tap your tummy and say 'maaa'.
3. Jump up – jump up and down and say 'maaa'. Really shake the sound out. Get it buzzing around your body. You could try some chanting if you're in a suitable place to do it!

Q: I feel very stiff after sitting at my desk and it makes it hard when I have to go and present to an audience. What can I do about this?

A: When we sit for a long time we close down the breath and tense the hips. This tension has an impact on your voice and your calm and it takes us into fight or flight response (see page 69). Warming up your body by doing some gentle stretches before you speak in public can help to relax your body and reduce your stress levels.

1. Stand on one leg and take the other leg in small circles – clockwise and anti-clockwise. Then swing the leg forward and back. (Lean on something for balance if you need to.)
2. When you return to standing, feel that the muscles around the hip and into the torso feel more relaxed and that your breathing has opened up as a result.
3. Swap sides, and repeat.
4. Now stand with your feet hip-width apart. Stand tall and imagine you are standing between two panes of glass.
5. Lift your arms over your head with your hands joined.
6. Bend to the left – think of lifting up and over, stretching the side of your body from head to toe. Imagine you are a cypress tree in the wind.
7. Now swap sides.
8. Notice how the breathing feels in the ribs afterwards and how the voice is freer.

Q: This new aligned posture doesn't feel natural to me, why is that?

A: The challenge with posture initially is habit. Cross your arms. Now cross them the other way. That feels weird, right? Anything beyond our habit feels unnatural at first. But if you keep crossing your arms the other way it starts to feel like a new normal. That's what we want to create, a new normal, and this will take some practice.

SUMMARY: VOICE NOTES

- Posture is key to a good voice because it creates a clear channel for sound and it allows you to find the confidence and energy of *hwyl*.
- Text neck – forward head posture is something to monitor as it has a bad effect on your voice (putting unnecessary tension into the voice and restricting breathing). Ears over shoulders is a good adjustment to text neck.
- Moving your body before you speak will relax you and make you more able to move and speak naturally.
- Good posture and alignment can build confidence, your metaphorical 'strong back and soft front'. The balance of softness and strength is key to good voices.
- Pilates, Alexander technique and yoga are all good disciplines to help you get these principles in the muscle.

CHAPTER FOUR

Speak Up and Stand Out: How to Find Your Confidence in the Moments That Matter

Courage is a heart word. The root of the word courage is cor - the Latin word for heart. In one of its earliest forms, the word courage meant 'To speak one's mind by telling all one's heart.' . . . Speaking from our hearts is what I think of as 'ordinary courage'.

BRENÉ BROWN, *I THOUGHT IT WAS JUST ME (BUT IT ISN'T)* (2007)

Your moment to speak up arrives. A space in the conversation looms, or you walk out on stage, or someone asks you a question. You have the opportunity to improve the silence, to contribute something new, to open minds. Do you apologise and stumble through your words? Or do you speak boldly and compel attention? These moments matter because when you speak up with confidence, people remember you.

You stand out. When you speak with self-awareness, empathy and a little boldness you create the right kind of visibility – a centred voice in a distracted world.

Your ability to speak up relies on the firm foundations we have been building at the lower levels of Maslow's hierarchy of needs. Speaking up and standing out is the big, bold step you make with those foundations in place. It requires the kind of trust in yourself that will allow you to dive into the moment and let go of your anxiety so that you can be there, present and listening, rather than lost in your head worrying.

This is not about flashy loudness; that's simply another way to present anxiety. What I'm talking about is self-actualisation: the top of Maslow's hierarchy. Maslow described some of the qualities of this kind of confidence: the ability to be independent, spontaneous and natural; to be able to laugh at yourself; to connect with others and to focus on a purpose beyond your own ego. To find your confidence, to truly self-actualise, you may need to override old conditioning that taught you to be perfect, to fit in, to sit down, to shut up. Self-actualisation is the zone where things get really interesting for you as a speaker: it's where you speak up, stand out and make change happen.

In this chapter we will think about:

- Why contributing, not competing, is the secret to speaking up and standing out.
- The art of conversational confidence and why listening is so important to it.
- Why you mustn't let 'perfect' be the enemy of confidence – and how to edit first, then express, so you keep your perfectionism in check.

- Work, rest and play: the three phases of 'speak up and stand out'.
- How to own your words.
- Tools to help you play with the voice and find your power.

Why You? Contribute Don't Compete

We are about contribution. It's not about impressing people. It's not about the next job. It's about contributing something. Did you do it better or worse than him ... I don't care ... Because in contribution there is no better. And what happens is the faces light up.

Ben Zander, conductor[1]

No one else can give you permission to speak as a grown-up. And you need to judge it right. You don't want to be the loud-mouth who dominates the room, while everyone else bristles. You don't want to be the silent ghost hovering at the edge, not daring to speak. You want to be the relaxed, focused, engaged contributor, who knows when and how to speak and, just as important, knows when to be silent. Aim to be the person who tunes in to speak in a way that lands with the room; the person who moves things on rather than repeating what's already known to the room. You want to be you: focused, calm, and centred.

But this can feel like a challenge when the pressure is on. If the stage is yours, how do you step into that moment with courage, owning your words, committing to what you believe?

If you need to speak up in a noisy room, how can you get a word in edgeways, persuade others to sit up and listen rather than ignore you, or talk over you? How can you be memorable, inspiring and convincing rather than getting tangled up in a heap of self-consciousness?

People get the moment of speaking up all wrong. They think it's about the 'Ta-da!!!', the 'look at me' moment. They think it's about impressing others. Modern life really doesn't help. It can ramp up the inner perfectionist to turbo mode. Every moment is a potential close-up, isn't it? The danger of this hyper-visual world is that we become a little too 'selfie-conscious', thinking about the perfect profile, the polished presentation, the just-so image. Our world makes us think in competitive terms – who gets the most likes is the most approved of, the most perfect. We think we have to be cool, polished, expert.

But this selfie-regarding culture, this need for likes and approval, sucks the life out of your voice, your independence and your confidence as a speaker. It will keep you small and flat as a speaker because you are censoring yourself, or worse it will make you loud and show off because you're desperate for approval. Neither of these approaches will make you stand out. We switch off as an audience when we listen to someone who is too quiet or who shows off. What works with an audience is calm, centred, self-aware confidence – the self-actualised kind. You, being you; with a reason to speak and without needing anyone else's approval.

Speaking up isn't about being the 'best' speaker; it's about moving things on. You can self-actualise all you like, but it's a solipsistic pursuit if it doesn't help anyone else. When you find your voice, get it out there. Make something better. Or what's the point?

If you want to speak up and stand out, forget competition. Focus on contributing instead. As Ben Zander put it, 'in contribution there is no better'. One of the characteristics of people who know when to speak up (and equally when to be silent) is that they are clear on what they contribute. When you know the answer to the question 'Why you?', then you know when to speak up and what to say. Your *why* gives you purpose and individual value in a room. Above all, the importance of your why – why you contribute – is that it allows you to listen to others without needing to compete because you offer something different, something which complements rather than overshadows. When you understand your why you can bring a specific note to the harmonies of the whole. You don't have to be the soloist in competition with everyone else.

Competing with others when you speak is a huge waste of energy. Not least because it stops you being a good speaker. When we are in competition we get stuck in a ratings game in our heads. Who is better? How do I sound? Competing prevents us from speaking up and being spontaneous, open and responsive. What you will be realising is that this competitive state is connected to the foe system (see page 83). So all the work you have been doing to help you relax into your calm centre (friend system, see page 81) will make your competitive self less likely to show up, and this is progress.

But old habits sometimes need conscious tweaking and when you are preparing for big moments (or little ones) it can really help to choose contribution over competition in your preparation and in your delivery.

How do you know if you are in competition with others?

- You feel stuck in your head and disconnected from the world.
- You hear the voices in your head (acting coach Viola Spolin called them the 'ghostly voices'[2] of your past) that tell you 'You can't do this', 'You're stupid', 'You're embarrassing', 'They're better than you'.
- You worry about what people will think, particularly whether they will like you and approve of you.
- You need the approval of others, and worry if you sense disapproval.
- You have success or failure thinking such as 'This is a disaster', 'I'm a failure'.
- You notice that you weigh yourself up against others – they're better, more expert, funnier. You feel separate.
- You find it hard to engage and empathise with an audience.
- You feel that you can't say what you think in case it's wrong, or you need to show off and impress people.

Stepping into contribution mode can help you find your voice in a flash. In recent years I have spent a lot of time in children's music classes with toddlers and their accompanying grown-ups. The aim of the classes is to create a love of music in the children yet I notice that very few of the adults join in and sing. Even in an environment where frankly no one really cares how cool or perfect you sound and where we are there to inspire the children, the adults don't sing; you have to ask what message that gives to the children? The adults have an editor in their heads that says where their voice is concerned that 'You are embarrassing, so be quiet'. Or 'You can't sing'. These are old messages you might have heard when you were much younger. But they don't need to torment you as an adult. You can override this editor. I see that in the music sessions so clearly. When it's a child's birthday and we are asked to sing 'Happy Birthday', everyone sings – because the moment is not about them. Just thinking of contribution can help to unlock your expressive self.

You Are Not Alone

In the big moments this sense of who you are speaking for, who you represent, is so important. You aren't a solo act. You have a tribe behind you, even if they aren't in the room. It can be a team, an organisation, a cause. Speak with this sense of contributing to the *we*, not the me. It's good for putting your worries into perspective, framing them in a bigger picture than your own psychodrama. Be in service to something bigger than you and your best self shows up immediately.

When you dive into contribution, and move beyond the anxious competing, you realise that all the worry was such a waste of time. No one is ever judging you as harshly as you judge yourself. Because the truth is that most people are thinking about themselves. When you approach speaking with a minute focus on your flaws, anxieties, on how you measure up, you are wasting good energy that can much more usefully be spent on how you can contribute to the moment. Confident speakers are not concerned with what they can get from the audience, they are focused on what they can give. And what you find when you focus on contribution rather than competition is that you dive into the experience rather than hold back.

There's a nervous moment for all of us when we hover on the edge of something. Do I dare to speak? Will I be accepted? Will others judge me? Am I good enough? Contribution neutralises all of that. It gives you permission to speak, to invite yourself, rather than waiting for the approval of others. It's such a breath of fresh air after the iron grip of anxiety.

When you focus on contribution, life becomes much more fun:

- You feel 'I can be me' here.
- You have a sense of parity - you show up as a respected equal, a fellow human rather than putting people high up on pedestals.
- You are relaxed with others, you connect and you welcome their success, because you are doing your own thing rather than competing.
- You have an understanding of the whole rather than just the parts. You know your why - what you specifically bring.
- You are present - to others.
- You have fun - time flies.
- There's little or no inner dialogue - your head is quiet.

Try This: Steps to Contribution

Everything you have learned about getting into your calm centre (see page 65) will help you learn how to have confidence to contribute. As a speaker the value of 'How can I help?' not 'How can I win?' is key, because that's where your creativity, compassion and energy as a speaker lives. When you are creative, compassionate and energetic, you express yourself with congruence.

Answering these questions can help you to show up with energy and to find your voice when it matters:

- Why you? Why does this matter to you? What's important here? What do you care about?
- What's your why? Who or what are you speaking for? Take a moment to identify your cause, your tribe, your team.
- What can you contribute? What can you bring to this meeting, party or event that no one else can? What will make you feel you are an equal? Draw on past memories of how you have contributed in the past and the difference that contribution made.
- What is your responsibility in this room? What do you bring in terms of vision and experience that no one else in the room can? What will no one else look after?
- What could happen if you *don't* speak? Can you identify the potential risk for the people you're speaking for if you don't speak up? Make a clear movie in your mind (see pages 100–101) of what could happen for

others if you don't speak. Speak up with a view to avoiding that future.

- What could happen if you *do* speak? Can you identify the potential reward for the people you're speaking for? Make a clear movie in your mind of a future where you have the change you want – see it, hear it, feel it. Work towards that future.

- What quality do you most want to show up with? Confidence? Fun? Authority? Calm? Lightness? Humour? Kindness? Or a mixture of all of them? Find ways to access these emotions within yourself. If you want the audience to feel excited, what makes you feel excited about this subject? Talk about it. Use the words 'I'm excited about . . .' Start to map in your mind what you want the audience to feel at each point in the talk, as it will impact what you say and how you say it.

Conversational Confidence

We've all been in presentations when someone's technology goes wrong in the middle of a boring slide deck. Have you noticed what happens? They jettison the tech and start to speak normally. Aren't these moments usually such a relief? Rather than turning their back, talking to their slides in flat tones, they start to look at you and talk, like a real human. Their eyes and their voices light up. They come back to life.

The effect of this sudden spontaneity is electric on an

audience. Our attention spikes in the presence of the spontaneous. What was dead and dull and totally predictable is now far more appealing to us. I suspect this was always true – that Shakespeare's audience really liked it when something went wrong on stage too. You can see it in contemporary comedy, theatre and music when a performer has to react to a sudden change, a heckle or something going wrong, and they break the fourth wall. The audience enjoys that moment when there is a connection with them. It's why performers say 'Never work with animals or children' – the unpredictable gets all the attention. You can use a balance of preparation and spontaneity to really up your game as a speaker, without needing to bring a menagerie on stage with you. Prepare enough that you can riff and you really become interesting to the audience.

Why does our attention spike when we see someone relax and speak conversationally? It's because we see someone confident enough to trust themselves to be spontaneous and not overly rehearsed. We love that they have the same tone, pace and resonance under pressure as they do in a normal conversation. It creates a sense of trust. We are wired to assess trust. When your tone is easy and conversational – when there's a harmony between what you are thinking and saying – the audience relaxes and listens. There's a congruence between your inner and outer worlds.

If the audience can't work you out, because your inner and your outer seem to be communicating different messages, they become uneasy. If you mumble or mutter, or try too hard to be polished and controlled, they wonder what you're hiding. So they stop listening and try to work you out, at least unconsciously. A voice that is too loud and too pushy, doesn't feel trustworthy. It suggests too much adrenalin, self-interest and a lack of empathy and connection with others. Equally, a voice that is too quiet or uncertain suggests a lack of confidence, an inability to fight someone's corner when it matters. But when you are conversational, confident, congruent, you have an audience's unreserved attention.

Conversational confidence matters more than ever. In the old days of public speaking – think lecterns, scripts, big hair and big stages – you could get away with a polished mask to hide behind. The world doesn't respond to that polish any more. It wants prepared spontaneity to deal with what arises on a 24-hour news cycle and rolling smartphone footage, rather than the perfectly set-up shot, look or soundbite. Platforms like TED and YouTube have changed what we expect from you as a speaker. We want you to seem relaxed and conversational, while at the same time being precise and prepared in your thinking.

Conversational quality is about ease. You need to give yourself permission to be the same you on the stage as the you who hangs out with your friends. It requires discipline, because ease in the spotlight takes a little work, just as ease in great cooking takes careful preparation. The surprise for most people is that being natural under pressure takes work, you can't just stroll on to the stage and expect it all to be wonderful. You need to prepare your message and plan carefully to feel natural in what can seem like an unnatural situation. Seeing something in the world is the first step to doing it yourself, so observe speakers you admire, who stay congruent and conversational in front of an audience and watch how they do it. You may notice that they are self-aware, calm, have good posture and are confident to speak up.

Start to think about how you can become more conversational in your big moments. It can help to visualise yourself speaking in this way in front of an audience – what do you see and hear on that screen in the ideal version? I do this when a speech or meeting is coming up that I feel nervous about. I consciously make a little movie clip in my mind of me in front of the audience smiling, enjoying it, being myself and notice the audience responding. The more you can visualise this conversational you, the more you can see yourself present, enjoying being in the moment with them, the easier it is to move towards that in your preparation. I visualise myself being really present to the audience, paying attention to individuals for a few seconds, seeing them responding and me reacting to their responses moment by moment, just as I do in a great conversation. This ability to listen and be physically present are key behaviours of great speakers.

Speaking is Listening

Good speakers are always good listeners first. When you see someone speaking with relaxed energy and variety of tone they are always listening. Listening is the fuel for your tone just as air is the fuel for your voice. It's why read speech sounds so different to speech in conversation. It's why the Q&A is where some speakers come to life, because they have to start listening, and stop reading.

This is why I want you to start to notice how you listen in conversations where you are really present and enjoying the moment. When you are having a relaxed chat with friends, your attention is on them. You aren't working out in your head what to say next. This is what brings your voice to life, because you are responding in the moment to what is happening. This quality is powerful on stage too. Though it seems different when a thousand people are staring at you, you can listen in exactly the same way. (This requires that your structure is very clear in your mind – see pages 167–171.) A good speaker absorbs the energy of the room, asks for questions and uses what the audience gives them all the time to keep the ideas alive.

You can listen to a roomful of people with the same calm and open attention as you listen to your friends. We think about speaking in the wrong way. We think it's all about broadcasting. It's not. Confident speakers are always having a conversation, even when it's them in the spotlight talking to 5,000 people. And you can have a conversation with minds and bodies, as much as voices. A confident speaker reads the feeling in the room and the mood of the audience to know what to say next and how to say it. They are able to listen moment by moment with their body as much as their ears. When you are listening to an audience you don't just notice what they say, you notice how they move. Are they rapt? Keep going. Are they fidgeting? Move on, change gear and ask a question. Listen, listen, listen and then your speaking will come alive.

FOUR LEVELS OF LISTENING

I love C. Otto Scharmer's four levels of listening model from his book *Theory U*.[3] We do these four kinds of listening perfectly naturally when we chat to someone and they are really useful to have as conscious choices for your attention when you speak.

Here are the four levels in detail:

Level 1 - download what you already know: At this level you confirm your existing knowledge of the audience, whether before the session or in the room. If they are finance types I might confirm my expectation that they are formal in style. If I'm with creatives I might confirm my expectation that they are a more relaxed crowd and that my style can be even more conversational.

Level 2 - notice what surprises you: Is there anything you hadn't expected about the audience? They might not behave the way you expected them to. You might get a question or a response you couldn't have planned for. If it challenges your world view, great. Be open to it (your calm centre preparation (see pages 82–83) will help you to do this). Take questions, enjoy the surprises, work with them – it ups your spontaneity in the room.

Level 3 - empathy: Step into the audience's shoes, tune into what they need. The more you are in your calm centre, the more you can pay attention to the audience and subtly adjust to what they need at each moment. Just like an ordinary conversation, you say something and then watch the other person process it. What's different to an ordinary conversation, of course, is that when you are the speaker in front of an audience, they probably aren't replying aloud to you. But you can look for a reaction from them as a group. As you speak, notice the mood of the room. Do they look thoughtful, curious, tired, stressed? Are they inspired? Do they need a break? Do they need to move, to energise? Ask yourself how it might feel to be them. A response to the audience in the moment is very compelling for listeners – it shows presence to the moment. You are tuning into the feeling of the whole room and responding to it. It requires that you are in your calm centre and able to really pay attention to the body language of your audience.

Level 4 - creative/generative listening: Here you read and respond to the room. This is what makes you really interesting and useful as a speaker, it's what Scharmer calls *generative listening.* It's your ability to tune in and to give them something that both delivers your planned speech and a bespoke response in the moment to what they need. This is where speaking comes to vivid life, because you are responding to what is actually happening and not simply trotting out the words you've rehearsed. It's an incredibly rich space. When you think that creativity so often comes when different perspectives meet, you realise that it's powerful to be able to riff with an audience.

Your calm centre and core confidence are the essential foundation to allow you to move between these four levels. When we get nervous we can get stuck in levels 1 and 2. I know I'm stuck when I find it hard to empathise, when I notice myself interrupting and finishing people's sentences. When this happens I tell myself to slow down, breathe and wait. This usually takes me into empathy (level 3) and from empathy I can usually become more generative (level 4) as I respond more deeply to the room. In those moments it's as if you and the audience are listening and speaking to each other in a big one-to-one conversation. It's a glorious feeling when you prepare your message and your calm centre to enable it. The work allows you to be light, conversational and easy. You read the room and you respond to it exactly as you would with friends. If you can be conversational with friends it's my firm belief you can be it with a thousand people. It allows you to speak up in a totally natural way and that relaxed confidence allows you to stand out.

Don't Edit Yourself as You Speak

One of the problems to finding our natural conversational ease as speakers is that we apply the same rules to writing as we do to speech. They are worlds apart, and you must understand the difference if you are to speak with confidence. Speaking is a flow of energy: fluid, changing, alive, imperfect. Writing is fixed on the page: perfect, finished. We learn a lot about the latter at school and we learn that success is about perfect words, getting our exam questions right. And so we apply that success strategy to speaking: be good, be right and be perfect. It doesn't work.

It was when I started to work with print journalists who wanted to be TV news reporters that I noticed that print journalists were trying to write in their brains as they spoke. At first I couldn't figure out why they found it hard to speak up and be congruent on camera. But it was because they needed to minutely control every word in their heads. It was taking their energy up into their heads, flattening their voices and making them robotic. The more anxious they felt, the more they tried to control their words and the more flat they sounded. I noticed them trying to edit what they said even as it was leaving their mouths.

It was the pursuit of perfect that was preventing them from speaking with confidence. I realised it was because these print reporters had trained for years to write the perfect phrase, the perfect headline, and they had assumed that this perfection was also required of them as speakers. But writing and speaking are not remotely the same. When we write we can edit, delete and cut and paste to our heart's content. We cannot do this when we speak. I was so sympathetic to them because as an actor I tried so hard to think my way to change – and my body didn't follow. Stress made me want to control things in my brain when the path to confidence was actually more about letting go. I think this is increasingly true for all of us. We are all able to hone our writing by cutting, pasting and moving ideas around on the page. Emails travel in neat, contained little boxes. We feel separate and controlled. But this isn't an effective strategy for confident speaking. It makes you flat and boring.

Self-editing and the quest to be perfect stop you from speaking up because you are worried you don't know enough, or that others know more. They stop you from speaking well because you're too busy listening to your inner censor trying to edit you mid-speech – 'You shouldn't have said that'. They stop you from trusting your instinct and responding in the moment.

If you want to speak up and stand out, forget perfect. Perfect is impossible anyway. We don't speak in perfect sentences (just look at a transcript of even the most eloquent speakers). Once the word is out, you can't take it back. Speaking is live. Holding back to edit what you are saying in your mind just makes you tentative and unimpressive. Be prepared, be present, trust your instinct and then commit to your choice.

Work, Rest and Play: the Three Phases of Speaking Up and Standing Out

How can you tell if someone is a truly confident speaker? Think of the speakers you admire and I will bet they have the ability to be both concise and conversational on the biggest of stages. They don't talk *at* an audience, they chat *with* them. There is a back and forth. They make eye contact. They connect conversationally.

How do they do this under pressure? They have a series of three phases that they complete: work, rest and play (this might sound familiar to you from the old advertising slogan).

Effective speakers first create great content. They *work* to get their content honed and edited so they are clear on their messages. Then they *rest* before they speak so the content can settle. So when they walk out in front of the audience they are able to relax and enjoy the moment, knowing all the prep is done and they can now focus on connecting with the audience. Their words are so clear that they can *play* and riff with the audience.

It's this combination of honed, concise words with relaxed

delivery that is the style of our age, popularised by all the video and podcast media our smartphones have enabled. If you want to find your conversational confidence you have to know how to do the hard work on your content so that you can then relax and find conversational ease in front of an audience. Too much effort and you can get stuck in your head. Too much ease and you are loose and unstructured, you don't contribute anything of value to the audience.

Conversational confidence gets the balance right between work and play. Though it looks spontaneous in the spotlight, that ease and playfulness is available to speakers precisely because they have a plan. When you have a clear sense of how you contribute and a plan of what you want to say, you are able to be natural. When it comes to preparing, do the work. You don't want to leave your content to chance.

	WORK	REST	PLAY
When	Before the speaking event (usually at least a week in advance if you can)	The night before, the morning of	In the moment of speaking
Behaviours	• Preparation • Rehearsal • Work hard	• Relax • Let the ideas settle • The half (see page 96) • Do nothing • No devices	• Playful • Relaxed • Expressive • Conversational • Enjoy the moment

Getting the Work Done

Let's look at what *work* means in this context. Whether you have five minutes or months, the process is the same. You need to create your content, plan your structure and rehearse it. Here's how.

MAKE IT YOURS

Original (adj) The origin or source of something; from which something springs, proceeds or is derived.

Original (n) A thing of singular or unique character; a person who is different to other people in an appealing or interesting way: a person of fresh initiative or inventive capacity.

Authenticity is one of the big words of our time. The days are gone when you could present a polished mask and a prepared speech and people were happy with that. Now we want to see *you*. It's a delicate balance to strike because I'd go as far as to say that there is authentic and then there is too authentic – we don't want to see the authentic you who loses your temper, or feels tired before a coffee, or needs a holiday. We want to see you on your A game, yet at the same time we want you to reveal a little of what makes you tick. I prefer the word *original* to authentic, the idea that the words you speak are words that only you could say because of the particular experiences that have brought you to this point. Originality makes what you have to say scarce and valuable to an audience, because they can only hear it from you. It means that you are able to keep generating new ideas, it gives you a real reason to speak, because you have something to contribute. It makes you stand out in a world where everyone consumes and very few people create their own new ideas. As a speaker, original ideas are the spark that will allow you not only to speak up with confidence but also to really stand out in a sea of sameness.

If you want to speak with confidence there's a really simple rule: create words you can own and feel proud of when you speak. Speaking with confidence has to start from within, just as voice does.

If you have ever sat through the painful experience of watching someone present material they haven't created you will have seen why originality matters: the person delivering words they haven't written; the person admiring someone else's work so much that they've just copied it wholesale. It's empty because it's not lived, oddly disembodied, a ventriloquist effect. The mouth is saying the words but the speaker doesn't own them. It's like a stand-up comedian delivering someone else's act. The words may still be funny but if they're not expressing a fundamental aliveness and experience of the world, they won't resonate in the same way. People can create a copy of a song – and it's usually a sign of success if they try to – but because they haven't lived the experience that created it, it will only ever be a cover version. Only you can bring your own material alive, because it comes from you. This means of course that if someone else asks you to present their material, you need to (gracefully) find a way to edit, tailor and make it yours.

So, if originality matters, how do you get the jumble of your thoughts in your head out to the world in a way that balances control and expression? This is a big question for most people. Your perfectionist editing brain needs to be given time to get the ideas in order so that it will feel safe enough to step back and let your expressive self let go and have fun on the day.

STRUCTURE YOUR THOUGHTS

You'll have lots of ideas for what you want to say, but you need to think about how to say them. Below is a really great structure for pulling together ideas, inspired by speech coach KC Baker.[4] She is a master at helping you structure your stories in a way that makes you feel that you can make your unique contribution.

Step 1: The Why

Get to the why – the heart of your message. Identify what you really want to say. Find a time when you feel relaxed and creative and have a go at answering the following questions.

- What's your purpose here?
- How can you honour the audience or the venue?
- Why does your message matter?
- Who do you want to help through this message?
- What motivates you to share these ideas? What's important about them?
- What stat/question/story could help you capture the audience's interest?

Step 2: I Believe

Why does what you are speaking about matter in the grand scheme of things? What do you believe is important for the audience to understand? Writing your beliefs down is such a brilliant exercise. It fires up your passion and sparks new thinking. I highly recommend it as your foundation for confident speaking.

Write down five times (or more):

I believe . . .
I believe . . .
I believe . . .
I believe . . .
I believe . . .

Then complete the sentence with what you believe about the subject you are focusing on. When you narrow down what you believe to be important, formed out of your experience, then you home in on your unique contribution.

Step 3: How can I help?

Now it's time to focus on the form your message will take. As a speaker it can help to think of yourself as being in the service of your audience. The more you help your audience in your talk, the more you and they will enjoy your speech.

The first step to getting to this point is to think about their challenges. Reflect on these questions below:

What's the key problem the audience face, and what have you learned that can help them to overcome it?

If you stood up and said the words 'If you do one thing . . .' to a group experiencing this particular challenge, how would you complete the sentence?

Step 4: Tell the story

What makes all the difference is taking time to go from the general to the specific – particularly with some great stories.

Think about key stories that bring to life the challenges that your audience face. They can be your stories or those of others. It helps to have stories about people who have faced these challenges and overcome them; there's lots of learning in that journey for your audience.

A good starting point can be research or data you've come across. You can usually connect it to a story to bring the facts to life.

It's fine to collect up too much material at this point; you can edit later.

Step 5: Transforming insight

What makes you most interesting as a speaker is your angle on the material, what you think about it. This generally comes from lived experience, your personal insight on the challenge and the shift in understanding and perspective it gave you in how to overcome it. This is where it's about contribution rather than competition. It's where you can speak up and stand out because you have something valuable to say.

This transforming insight is the engine of your expertise on stage. It gives you a right to speak, an ownership of your material.

So, what is the key transforming insight that changed your thinking about the problem and how you deal with it? When did you learn this? What happened as a result of this insight?

Think about moments in your life where you have learned new ways to handle the challenge that you are focused on in the speech.

Take one of those moments. Delve into it. How can you bring that moment alive for the audience? What would you do if you were creating it as a movie? What was the epiphany? What changed? What did you understand differently?

Step 6: How to give your audience the key steps to success

Now you've outlined the key challenges and the insight that can help the audience overcome them, you can share your expertise that will help them really step up in their lives. This is where your talk adds practical value, as well as inspiring them.

- What can you make visible for them that without you they would not have seen?
- How can they use this in their lives?
- What benefit will it give them?
- What will change in their lives, businesses, in the world?

Be generous and share your secrets where possible so your listeners can really make changes in their lives. Refine your thinking down into three–five steps that your audience can follow. Imagine teaching a friend how to do them. Sum it all up into an 'If you do one thing . . .' sentence. This gives you a real distillation of your message.

Step 7: Close powerfully

Try the following:

- Return to your challenge story and close the loop.
- Go back to an initial quote or number with the new learning in mind.
- Remind the audience of the transforming insight.
- Give a memorable metaphor or phrase.
- Tell a short story that inspires and summarises the theme.
- Ask a question.
- Loop back to a question you asked earlier and answer it.

Step 8: Signposts

Now go back over the notes you have made and find the *signposts* – the absolute essentials of the structure.

Write these signposts as single images or words on sticky notes. We are now going to look at how you can take these sticky notes and create a mind map.

MAP YOUR THINKING

The balance between a plan and spontaneity, between control and expression, is fundamental to confident speaking. When you are confident you can riff around a tune. As any jazz musician will tell you, you can only improvise around a tune you know really well. When you have prepared and rehearsed what you are going to say, you have control and you can then allow your personal expression to come out. You become the speaker who looks totally natural and on point.

Most people at this stage either write a script or create PowerPoint slides. I want to steer you away from both.

The trouble with a script is that it makes you feel that you are writing an essay. You are being diligent but it's so hard to bring a speech alive off the page and it makes most people very nervous because they read the whole thing verbatim. So your eyes look down, your voice goes flat and you use a reading voice with a sing-song tone that sends the audience to sleep or to their emails.

The issue with using slides is that your slides aren't for you – they are for the audience. If you load up your slides as your script, or create slides and then dump your script on notes pages, then you will either be tempted to stare at your screen as you speak, or read off your notes pages on a monitor, paper or your device.

Please don't use either of these methods. If you are staring at a script or a screen you have lost connection with the audience. They want you to be conversational, human, yourself. Conversations are not fun when someone is reading from a phone or a piece of paper. With my hand on my heart I urge you to step away from the script. Step away from the slides. Instead, create a *mind map*, which shows the flow of your thinking clear on one page.

What is a mind map? It's a brilliantly simple creative tool

(created by the late Tony Buzan) to help you lay out your ideas visually on one page. Mind maps work because they give you structure and creativity, a very good combination for speaking with conversational confidence. The brain likes to radiate and organise ideas spatially. The mind map works with that because the ideas branch out from a central point, organised in a clockwise direction, which helps you think them through and figure out your timings. The brain also likes colour, so in a mind map make each section of your speech a different colour and draw pictures of key images to help you remember them.

With this mind map you can lead the audience through your original thinking with calmness and control. You won't tangle yourself up in knots. There will be a clear thread from your brain to your mouth, because you have everything you need to say clearly, colourfully and visually on one page. You will have your main ideas, the links and the timings laid out in front of you. You will walk out on stage and literally have your speech in the palm of your hand. I can't tell you how much nicer that is than staring down at a shaking script in your hand and frantically wondering how you find your place again. Or having no clue what the next slide is before you click on it so you make up something random that doesn't segue. Once you've written a map and made it colourful and visual it is memorable. When the signposts are clear in your head you will find that you can put the map down and just talk, which is ultimately the key to speaking with confidence.

MIND-MAP FIRST

If you really feel that you need to use PowerPoint or a script, mind-map first then create the deck and script. A mind map allows ideas to grow organically whereas a script locks them – and you – in.

Try This: How to Draw a Mind Map

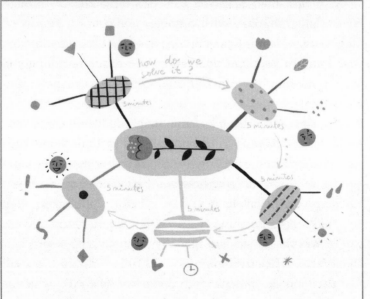

I'm going to use the example of giving a talk on how to find your voice to show you how to draw a mind map.

1. Take a sheet of paper and coloured pens. Lay the paper landscape.

2. At the centre of the paper (leaving lots of space for your map around it) draw an image in three colours that symbolises your subject. You can give this image a word if that helps you.

3. Think of how many sections you need in your talk (you'll always need an introduction and a conclusion). Draw a line for each section from the central image, like the spokes of a wheel. Each line should be in a different colour so that you can clearly separate the sections in your head. Always work in a clockwise direction.

4. At the end of each line, give each section an image and title (limit yourself to the absolute minimum number of words). These are the signposts of your talk.

5. Now add lines off your main spokes with the key points and images you need for each section. Three key points per section are usually more than enough. Keep them simple – a single word or image. You can number them if it helps.

6. Create links between the main sections – these are the words you will say between each idea, for example: 'So, if that's the problem, how do we solve it?' These links can be drawn as arrows, with a word that sums up the link.

7. It is also useful to add timings for each section. If, for example, you have 30 minutes to speak and have five

sections to cover, then you know you need to keep each section to five minutes or so, leaving five minutes in hand to deal with questions or the unexpected.

8. Finally, decide how you want the audience to feel in each section: excited, curious, worried, inspired, etc. Write this on the map, or add a picture that suggests the emotion (a smiley face is often a simple cue). This reminds you to consciously find these emotions as a speaker.

REHEARSE

Once you have crafted your content, you have to rehearse. Thinking about the words isn't enough. Rehearsing in your head isn't enough. Until you've said the words out loud a few times to yourself, and ideally to someone else, you've really just written an essay. Speaking is physical. You have to get the words in the muscle. Rehearsal creates memory in the body that allows you to be instinctive and playful in front of an audience rather than having to overthink every word. Think about anything physical that you've learned to do, from driving to dancing. You've learned it through rehearsal, practice and repetition. Lay down new habits so you can then get them in the muscle and be instinctive in the moment.

The cost of not rehearsing is that the audience have to watch you working it out in front of them. Warming up in front of an audience this way is a cardinal sin of performers.

The first few minutes are vital to the impression you make as a speaker. It's painful to watch someone slowly getting up to full speed about five minutes in. So, take control. Book sacrosanct time in your diary before a meeting or speech to think, prepare and rehearse (see page 96 for information on the half). If you have said the words aloud before you speak them to the audience you will feel calmer, readier and your system will feel safer (see pages 90–95) because you have a back-up drive in your brain. It can be far easier than you realise to rehearse, it's simply a matter of speaking the words aloud a few times before you say them to the audience. You can do the first few run-throughs sitting on the sofa or in the garden. Then you will benefit from one or two rehearsals in front of a camera or person you trust.

Practise until you know your beginning, your signposts and your ending, so you have at your fingertips the key points through the journey of your message. Then you can use them to orient yourself at any time when you need them as you will know how to get from one signpost to the next. This gives you ownership of your words and that easy conversational confidence. You don't have to memorise your speech word for word. When you have done enough work you will know. When you are clear on your message you speak up with ease and openness, trusting yourself to read the room. Then you really stand out.

Rest: Let the Work Sink In

Finding your voice and learning to speak with confidence are essentially creative processes. In order to be creative you need downtime. Once you have created your mind map and run it through a few times, there is enormous value in doing 'nothing' for a while. You need to let go of the editor in your brain and take some time out. You know your schedule and the value of the message. Let the message sink in overnight. Give yourself a break. Do something fun. Clear your conscious mind and find your calm. Let your unconscious work for you in the background. Find the dream time that really sparks up your originality.

Try This: Say Thank You to Your Inner Editor

If for whatever reason your brain won't quieten down, just say 'Thank you' and notice how a little appreciation usually encourages it to go quiet. Your system is trying to help you out, for all the reasons we explored in Chapter Two. It thinks you need to fight, run or hide and is effectively giving you a pep talk to get you out of there. By saying thank you, you help your editor understand that its work is done and that it can stand down and let you have fun and be playful and expressive with the audience.

Have an early night before your big moment to rest your body and mind. Do something relaxing to help your body get a great night's sleep. Any of the breathing exercises on pages 94–96 will help. I particularly like to use the Weight Your Diaphragm exercise (see pages 43–46).

Know what gets your engine running: yoga, going for a run,

sitting quietly and relaxing to music, it's different for everyone. What you definitely won't be doing is checking emails and messages or paying attention to other people's agendas (see pages 74–75). Make the time yours so you can let the work settle and get ready.

Play: Find the Fun

Once you've done the work, taken a rest, you can play. Finding ways to be playful, to bring fun, energy and dynamism to your voice is important as they give you the freedom to speak up and stand out.

Speaking up with confidence is a little like driving in city traffic. You have to be bold or you simply won't get anywhere. The trouble is that life knocks the boldness out of us. We experience knockbacks, criticism and judgement and therefore we can tell ourselves that it's better not to speak up, that it's less risky to stay small and safe and keep the approval of others. Now, this may have worked in the past, but the contemporary world doesn't value safe and small. It values bold, playful, confident and authentic. I want you to be all of these things when you need to own a room.

Fun allows you to dive into the moment, to be expressive; that's when you stand out. You open up the creative part of you. It's where your energy, your charisma, your presence are. You relax, you connect and you open up. If you are in front of very serious people, it can be serious fun, contained to a glint in your eyes with power in your voice. When you are with a lighter-hearted crowd, go for it. Enjoy yourself.

Share Your Voice

When you have something worthwhile to contribute, you will want to make it heard. That's when you need to know how to share your voice. When you've got something good to say you don't want to swallow your voice in your throat and mumble your words. You want to let it out. You want to contribute energy as well as ideas to the room. That's what we will be thinking about here.

Of course it takes a little boldness. But it's so worth it. Energy is infectious. When you give an audience the energy that is right for the moment, that energy comes back to you like a boomerang. Then it feels easy. But at first you have to take the leap. Trust your preparation and go for it.

Let me take you to a library space in central London on a spring morning. Fifteen talented women in film are here to find the voices that will give them resonance in their professional sphere. We are doing an exercise called 'Speakers' corner'. We start to walk around the room in different directions, hyper-aware of each other. Each person stops at the moment that feels right to them, and we come to a stop with them. We wait. When they are ready they speak, they say their name (so often a hard thing to say to a group without rushing). They each say: 'I am [name] and I am here.' It's a moment of heightened visibility and each of them meets it differently.

They hold on to their voices in totally normal ways – a normal response to anxiety, of being in a new situation. Some are quiet and their voices don't travel far across the room, or they lack the range that will hold our attention. Some speak fast and gallop through their words. Some uptalk (see page 189), sounding a little apologetic for their presence.

What I know is that with some simple tweaks we can sound-engineer their voices so an energised and energising sound pours out of them, spiking our attention as an audience.

What follows are some simple ways to share your voice, and they have been known to you since you played with your voice as a small child. They are definitely to be done in the privacy of your own space, not in front of an audience!

Open Your Mouth

You need to open up your mouth to open up your sound. Remember that resonance is the vibration of voice passing through amplifying spaces (see page 47). The space above your larynx is the primary bony cavity for resonance and the more you open up the space, the more the sound can resonate.

1. Make a big face – eyes wide open, mouth wide open and do a large, open stretch. Doing a big yawn can help you find this.
2. Then use all that space in your mouth to speak. Notice the sound flows out of you.

HELP YOUR MOUTH TO OPEN

Some voice teachers swear by what's called a 'bone prop' to help you open your mouth - they stick between the teeth so you can practise speaking with the space. You can order them online. Others recommend placing a wine bottle cork between the teeth. Whatever works for you to find space between the teeth as you speak.

Wake Up Your Range

Some voices glide and scoop with a natural range that makes you love listening to them. The voice is so much about music. Think of calling for someone for a few minutes: first excited, then puzzled, then angry, then worried. Each time you call the name your pitch changes, it's the pitch that expresses the meaning. The trouble is that we lock our voices down when we go into fight or flight or have low vagal tone (see page 91), so it can be helpful to bring your natural range and music to your voice before you speak to an audience. It's like a musician warming up before they play. If you have accessed more of the notes in your voice by, say, singing along to some music, then when you speak to an audience your voice will naturally glide up and down more without you having to think about it.

Freeing up your range is really a matter of getting the vocal folds to wake up and stretch (see pages 28-30).

Playing with range in this way is helpful in lifting your mood too before you speak. You can sing at home beforehand. Or in the car. It's about waking up the voice and body. When you find more of your natural, playful range in your voice it keeps an audience awake and interested too.

- Putting some music on that you love and singing along is a brilliant way to get your voice open and energy moving.
- A simple way to find range is to take your hand up in the air and find a high note on a 'mmm' or 'nngggg'. Then gradually let your hand drop and go down your range. Move your hand up and down a few times and let the pitch follow.
- Do something to loosen up the body before you speak. There are lots of suggestions in Chapter Three. Choose the exercises that work for you and do them at home in the morning.

Inside Voice, Outside Voice: How to Fill a Room with Ease

Why not use your outside voice? You know I sometimes think the most effective people in the world are introverts who taught themselves to be extroverts.

Meg Wolitzer, *The Female Persuasion* (2018)

Confident, expressive voices benefit from some boldness in the delivery. This is where it helps enormously to understand how to project your voice. Then you can own your words with ease. What you need to understand is the difference between your *inside voice* and *outside voice*. Inside voice is quiet, intimate, one to one. Outside voice has a relaxed, open resonance that easily fills a room. The voice that will allow you to be heard is an outside voice that has an easy, centred power. It's the voice that calls 'Hi!' with delight across a garden to an old friend. The voice that can easily fill a room, welcoming people to an event. It's a voice that feels as if it's hugging you with energy. Some people don't use their outside voice in their spotlight moments because they don't want to be seen as too big, too pushy.

I understand that it can feel difficult. Cutting into a room full of loud voices can be daunting, even when you know you have something worth saying. You can't get a word in edgeways because they're all so loud. Or you try to cut into the conversation and a mouse squeak emerges out of you, so people talk over you, or pick up your idea and run with it and get all the credit. It can be so disheartening that you then sit back in a secret vow of silence. But sitting out of the conversation can be equally frustrating, especially if it takes a turn you don't agree with.

If we all lived in wide, open spaces, we would mostly have the ability to have wide, open voices. Our bodies, our voices, have an inherited muscle memory of calling across large spaces. We didn't evolve in offices, cars and lifts. Just the act of imagining that you are in a wide, open space, looking out on a vast horizon, with soft grass under your feet, can have a huge impact on your voice and body language: your voice will be open, relaxed and have an easy projection. After a day in a small meeting room, or a silent, open-plan office, you will notice the opposite: a little voice that struggles to fill space. It is important to understand that these are habits. You can change the habit of speaking only in inside voice and learn to find your outside voice when you need to speak up for something you care about, or connect with a larger group of people.

To be heard, you must commit. Think about driving. If you are too tentative, no one will make way for you. If you nose out into the traffic confidently and respectfully, people will make way. When you are bold and committed people make space for you because you have already made space for yourself.

Try This: Find Your Inner Volume Control

If you want to share your voice fully with an audience you need to find your support muscles, which give you your inner volume control. They support the column of air going out of your body which creates volume (see pages 186-187). They are the same postural muscles low down that we found on pages 117-120, and these exercises teach you how to use them effectively.

To find the postural muscles a really simple thing to do is squeeze the palms of your hands together at diaphragm height. Or you can do a yoga prayer position, or press one palm on top of the other. Can you feel the muscles low down in your torso as you squeeze? If you talk now you will feel these muscles support your sound from low down too. These are the deep support muscles that give your voice power.

- A simple way to reconnect to these muscles that support your volume is to do a controlled 'ssssssss' sound, squeezing the sound out of you, like toothpaste from a tube, from the bottom first, then core and stomach, then ribs.

- If you prefer, you can also test this with a straw and a glass of water. Blow air through the straw into the water to make bubbles and hum as you do this. Can you feel the muscles around your stomach, ribs and the inner muscle of the diaphragm supporting the lungs squeeze the air out? Those muscles will give you projection power. Notice that if you squeeze the lower support muscles harder you have more bubbles (just like blowing up a balloon). This is volume - air pressure is volume.

- Now use these muscles to give you effortless power. Open up your arms wide and with a lovely open yawn feeling in the throat send out a big expansive 'Heyyyyy' as if you are greeting a friend in another room in your house or across a field. Keep your mouth open and smiling and notice how you are able to extend the sound easily. The aim is that the throat stays open, you are relaxed and smiling, and the work happens low down.

- To play with volume control you squeeze and release the muscles. Make a 'VVvvVVVvvVVV' or 'shSHshSH-shSH' sound like a revving motorbike and feel those low muscles squeeze and release. Remember that volume is air pressure. The more you squeeze air out the more volume you create. To power up you simply squeeze more air pressure out with the lower support muscles. As a general rule you want to feel these lower support muscles helping you out all the time.

Projection Without Push

Filling a room with your voice is much easier than you realise. Once you have found your inner volume control, projection is simple.

Think about the action of throwing. When you throw a ball, the whole body is involved. You have a clear sense of direction. You identify where you are throwing to. You make eye contact with the person you are throwing to. You connect to your core, breathe in and throw on the out-breath. Throwing, or projecting, your voice works in the same way. It is the sending of a thought, powered by the body. The voice becomes a projectile.

The secret to easy projection is to have a physical sense of where you need your voice to travel to – i.e. the back wall. It can help to look at people at the back when you start off, so you begin strongly. Then keep your voice travelling to the back of the room, even as your eyes find people in other parts of the room to make a few seconds of conversational eye contact with. If you have a sense of always speaking to the furthest wall and send your voice there, it will power up.

Try This: Pull the Sound In

To get a sense of speaking to the furthest wall, there's a classic exercise which requires you to *pull* your voice into you. It works because it feels so much less effortful to pull your voice in than to push it out, it gives you a grounded power. After practising this exercise a few times you can keep in mind the feeling of always pulling your voice into you when you speak.

1. Find a quiet space. Try the exercise standing first (then you can always try it sitting).
2. Attach an imaginary piece of string to the furthest wall, or to a point out of the window, and pull it into you with your left arm as you say 'Monday'. Pull your arm into your stomach as you speak.
3. Then pull in the string with your right arm and say 'Tuesday'.
4. Keep going through the days of the week, swapping arms each time. Notice how it ups your power. The more volume you want, the further you reach and then pull that piece of string.

The Way You Say It

> It was always so much easier to turn a statement into a question, because in the end you could backpedal and say you were only asking, and then you wouldn't have to endure the shame of being wrong.
>
> Meg Wolitzer, *The Female Persuasion* (2018)

So you have something great to contribute. You know your why. You know your who. You have mapped your message. So why does the how feel so difficult sometimes? We undercut the importance of what we are saying and why we matter, by the way we say it. In this section we're going to look at some of the common speech characteristics that undermine your message and make you sound less confident when you speak.

Uptalk

Uptalk is when the voice goes up in tone at the end of a sentence so that it sounds like a question and this takes away the power of your voice. It conveys a lack of certainty and so other speakers or colleagues get worried about you and cut in or interrupt. So why do we uptalk? It has a positive intention which is to reflect, to seek approval and consensus. And in situations where you are exploring, and are with people who want to do the same, and don't mind uncertainty, it's okay. It's also fine in situations where connection is more important than authority. But these uptalk intonation patterns are problematic in situations where the audience need you to sound more certain. In those moments your uptalk is an invitation for others to interrupt and talk over you.

A simple psychological way to banish uptalk is to remember that sometimes it doesn't matter if those who are listening to you like you or not. Uptalk is often about approval-/liking-seeking and you may not need approval or to be liked. What if in those situations you focus on being respected instead? When you walk into the room with a clear sense of common purpose then you may find that if you keep the goal in mind that you don't need to apologise or ask for permission to speak. You can own it because you are speaking for something bigger than you.

(See Try This: Bricks in the Wall on pages 191–192 to help you with uptalking.)

Tailing Off

Do you sometimes tail off at the ends of sentences? This happens for a few reasons: because you are thinking about the next line; because you want reassurance from others that your ideas are okay; because you haven't given yourself space to breathe between each thought (see pages 88–90). Speech can be such a giveaway, can't it? Breath usually follows our thinking and when your thinking is uncertain the breath and the voice reveal you. And when you let the energy die at the end of your sentences, the audience feel like they want to die after a few minutes of this too. The answer is to finish each thought firmly before you start thinking about the next one. The exercise below will help with this (as well as with uptalk). The stronger you land the end of a sentence, the more firm you feel and the less you go up in tone or tail off in energy. Commit to each sentence and your confidence will follow.

Try This: Bricks in the Wall

This is a really helpful exercise to support you in driving energy to the end of the line and giving the ends of sentences an extra punch. The trick is to really place the words, particularly the meaning words of the sentence, and the last word of the line. This stops you tailing off on to another thought, which can make you sound very uncertain. If it helps, think of the way a newsreader goes slightly down in tone at the end of the line and drives the last word of the sentence - 'Here is the *news*' - to help you cut out the rising inflection of uncertainty or the tailing off in energy.

1. Take an imaginary brick from the floor (yes, really). You are going to say the days of the week and I want you to drop the brick on 'Monday'. Notice how the voice tails off.

2. Say the days of the week again but this time throw the brick up in the air on 'Monday' and feel the tone go into the uptalk lift in intonation.

3. Now take the brick and visualise a wall in front of you with a brick-shaped hole. Say the days of the week again and as you get to 'Sunday', place the brick carefully in the hole. Notice it makes you commit to the sound. You are bolder, more confident and more impactful.

4. Think about this exercise when you speak, put bricks in the wall and drive the energy to the end of each sentence. Notice how people listen differently when you make space for the words in this way. Give every word the connection and space it needs.

A NOTE ON SCRIPTS

As I've mentioned previously, I recommend that you don't use a script. But if you have to, make sure you obey the 'eyes up at the end of the line' rule. As soon as your eyes go down to the script your voice tone and energy drop off.

Banish Your Modifiers and 'Um's

Modifiers pepper our language and as the word suggests, they modify what we mean and weaken our message. No 'try', no 'I'm just, sorry, no', no 'might'. Modifiers are banned. Cut them out of your language. Also banish 'um's.

If you recognise that you like to use modifiers and 'um's, get someone to count them for you in your next meeting. It's amazing how quickly you can cut them out when you become aware of them. Put a brick in the wall (see page 191) at the end of each sentence and close your mouth to prevent them forming. A pause is infinitely preferable on the whole.

There's No Need to Rush

When you are speaking you are responsible for the audience's mood and energy. Rushing stresses them out. It is much better to give them one idea at a time and let them think about each idea, rather than rushing them through.

Resist the urge to rush. Don't go at the pace of your brain. Go at the pace of the audience. Think each thought with the audience, as if you haven't thought about it before. Make sure you have something worth listening to and then say it fully and with energy. Really enjoying clear, muscular speech is the best way to achieve this. If you use your articulators fully (see page 53) and speak with muscularity, it's very hard to rush. You make each word count. And audiences will pay attention. This is even more important these days when you are likely to be on international calls or speaking to big groups made up of different nationalities. In these moments, getting the sounds shaped clearly matters even more.

The best kind of energy when you speak is controlled and powerful. People make the mistake of conflating speed with energy. Fast speech is like the wheels of a bike are spinning but you're going nowhere. As any cyclist will tell you, you have to have power. And power comes when you slow down slightly, because you can give each word more cadence, more energy.

Try This: Clear, Muscular Speech

Voice coach Cicely Berry's exercises are brilliant as her love of language comes through in them.[5] Here are some of her exercises. Do them before you speak to get your mouth moving around the words.

1. Take some words you need to speak and whisper them - feel your mouth shape each sound. Overdo it.
2. Say the word with just the consonants, take all the vowels out. Exaggerate, let your mouth really shape them.
3. Then just say the vowels, go to town on them.
4. Put the word back together and feel how you really make shape for the sounds. You have muscularity.

DOES ACCENT MATTER?

If you speak with clarity, muscularity, controlled pace and put your bricks in the wall, your accent will be easy to understand, whoever your audience. It can be a good idea to cut out any words in dialect or jargon, then you will find that, in most places, the accent you speak with is an irrelevance.

Speaking Up and Standing Out Can Be Fun

'Public speaking' is a term I would banish to the history books. I loathe it. It makes speaking sound so un-fun. It brings to mind lecterns and bellowing and boring broadcast speechifying. Forget it. Let's just call it speaking, with a plan, a calm mind, a confident voice and your natural energy and passion. Follow the advice in this book and you will find that you can be you, with added oomph and power, when you speak. And that it can be fun. When you enjoy it the audience tend to enjoy it too and come away inspired and ready to take action.

I tell you this because I know what it's like to worry about public speaking and to turn it into something serious and daunting. Look, I'm an introvert. A bold introvert perhaps, but I'm really never happier than sitting quietly with a great book and a sea view. So speaking up and standing out should in theory be my idea of hell. But it's not any more. I can say to you, hand on heart, that I have learned to have fun as a speaker. I work hard on the content, I care for my voice, my calm, my energy and then I dive into the performance and focus on making the experience fun and useful for the audience. I have learned that speaking can be fun.

Because your voice is the expression of your aliveness, because your voice is you, you may well find that as these new skills become new habits, they help your confidence beyond speaking. I came to realise this recently. Twenty years ago I had to do one of those classic drama school trust exercises where you stand on a wall and fall backwards, to be caught by the out-stretched arms of your classmates. I really hated that exercise. I tensed up, held my breath, worried they'd drop me.

Twenty-plus years later, I found myself standing on a wall and with no warning was required to stage-dive into a large crowd in an immersive theatre production in London. I relished how different the experience felt. Yes, I felt the rush of the foe system as it processed a potential threat. But I relaxed my breathing, strengthened my core, found a sense of fun and excitement in the adrenalin, trusted and fell backwards on to 20 outstretched arms and they carried me across the crowd. It was an amazing feeling that I still feel lifted by. And that feeling, that ability to dive in, is what I want for you as a speaker. Prepare. Centre. Dive in. The audience will catch you.

Your Questions

Q: How can I up my energy when I speak?

A: Before a big meeting, event, performance or even a party where you want to speak up and stand out, put some great music on and sing along.

Smile. Think of a great secret or a very happy memory. Let it reach your eyes and notice the feeling in the back of your throat – this can up your energy even if people can't see it. It lightens your voice and expression and lifts the audience at the same time.

Remember the power of your big toe (see Front Foot Energy on pages 121–122).

Q: How do I speak up in meetings?

A: First be clear on what you can contribute. If you are confident in your area of expertise it's much easier to know when to speak up. It may help to have a clear sense of who you are speaking for or a subject area in mind that you know you will speak up about when the moment comes.

Make sure you are speaking for the right reason. Check you are calm – the foe zone can make you want to show off or interrupt. Make sure your contribution will move things forward.

When the moment is right, commit and then project your voice to the back wall. Keep your words concise. Land them well and you will stand out and be remembered for all the right reasons.

If someone interrupts you or disagrees, use the 'yes and' technique: Say 'Thanks [their name], yes, [then reference their words positively] and . . . [you continue].

Q: How do I make eye contact with a big audience?

A: I like the bumble bee technique. Imagine the audience is a garden. Divide the room into quadrants. Think of your eye contact like a bee landing on a flower and give each quadrant equal attention in random order like a bee landing on a flower. Choose a flower at a time to send eye contact to.

Q: I don't like phone meetings – any tips?

A: So many people hate talking on the phone: it's a weirdly disembodied experience and you don't get enough feedback to tell you how you are doing. The answer is to picture the person on the other end of the line. Picture their face. Picture where they are sitting. See their smile and smile back as it will make your voice warmer. Allow longer pauses, this can help with time or signal delays – you don't have to jump to fill every pause. Speak clearly and with power. Standing up can really help give you confidence. Gesturing will give you vocal energy. Above all focus on them not you: listen, listen listen.

Q: How do I end my talk?

A: The last few lines of your talk should be strong. When you are totally finished speaking, pause, connect to the audience, pause and say 'Thank you'. Smile and stay still as they applaud.

SUMMARY: VOICE NOTES

- Speaking up and standing out is so much easier when you know your why. Clarify how you can contribute. When you know you can contribute, give yourself permission to speak up confidently.
- The best speakers have conversational confidence, delivering a prepared, concise message with relaxed spontaneity. What this enables above all is listening. Use the four levels of listening to help you.
- Work, rest and play. Do the work on the content, rehearse so it's comfortable and in the muscle, then take a break, let the ideas settle. Knowing you are ready, trust your process, dive in and be playful.

- Mind maps are useful tools for planning in a way that enables control and expression. Use them whenever you can.
- Be bold, use your outside voice.
- Learn how to minimise speech characteristics that can undermine your message: tailing off, uptalking, using modifiers, rushing.
- Speaking can be fun!

CHAPTER FIVE

Strong Back, Soft Front

What kind of mind and heart can stay so strong and
open in the midst of all this chaos?

JOAN HALIFAX, *BEING WITH DYING* [1997]

Let's think about the journey we've taken to help you find
your voice and speak with confidence, drawing on Maslow's
hierarchy of needs (see pages 13–14). In a world that is
fast-moving and distracted there's little that's more important than learning to trust and settle into your voice. We've
planted deep roots in the body so that your voice and confidence can flourish and grow.

Below is a summary of the main steps in the hierarchy
we've explored so that you can come back to them and keep
integrating them into your mind–body–voice.

Chapter 1: We started with what Maslow called *physiologi-
cal needs*, via your awareness of **Your Incredible Instrument**.
We explored how the voice works, building your curiosity

and awareness so that you know how to care for your voice and can feed it the core nutrients of good posture and relaxed breath support. When you pay your voice relaxed attention it becomes a supportive friend rather than an unpredictable stranger. *Remember that the voice is an instrument, the in-breath is your inspiration and thinking time, and the out-breath is where you speak. Know that the voice is the best way to steward your nervous system to calm with this awareness.*

Chapter 2: We moved up to the second level of the hierarchy, *safety needs*, to **Find Your Calm Centre.** You learned that rather than speaking being a stressful experience, you can actually calm your system down when you speak by minimising the gasp and taking a low, wide breath. You also have the ability to find a conscious sense of *love and belonging*, the third level of the hierarchy, from within with the help of the vagus nerve and the good habit of the half. When you know how to find this calm, connected centre you can use adrenalin to boost you instead of it overwhelming you. You can speak with confidence and calm in the highest-stake moments with these good habits in the muscle. *Remember the power of the half and a long out-breath to calm you wherever you are. Talk to 'old friends' as a fast route into connection.*

Chapter 3: With those deep supportive roots in place I showed you how to build *esteem*, as Maslow called it, giving you new habits to strengthen your core confidence via the body. **Get Out of Your Head** is about knowing that your body is key to

confident speech. Remember that good posture is fundamental to your confidence. It allows the diaphragm to move
freely and communicates strength and stability to your own
system and to others. *Minimise text neck by keeping your
gadgets under control and remember 'ears over shoulders'
and 'strong back, soft front'.*

Chapter 4: Finally, with the strong foundation of the body
and breath in place, we explored *self-actualisation*, at the top
of hierarchy, your ability to speak up with confidence in tricky
moments. This is to enable you to **Speak Up and Stand Out.**
The more that you can connect to your why and your ability
to contribute rather than compete, the more you will feel able
to find your voice and speak with confidence. *Remember that
confidence will be there for you spontaneously when you get
your message so clear and concise that there is space to listen. And when you speak be bold – get your voice out there
into the world.*

Me to We

Out beyond ideas of wrong-doing and right-doing there is a
field. I'll meet you there.

Rumi, Sufi mystic and poet

One of the things I always notice after a voice class, or after
my choir, is that when our voices come together the room is
changed by the sound. You feel the sound buzz in the room,

even after the end of the song. When you voice it travels out beyond you, vibrating air molecules travelling out across space. An open resonant voice, powered out of your strong core on the breath, has a reach way beyond your arm span. When you open up your voice and find your easy, natural sound you create a buzz in the room.

At a time where we all seem locked in – to our heads, to our devices, to our psychodrama/world view, to our construct of independent self – what I love about the voice is it quite literally transcends you. Voice is energy. When you speak you are creating something that has already travelled beyond you. Voice travels. Voice connects. Voice bridges. Voice transcends. The air that makes your larynx vibrate, in turn makes the ear of your listener vibrate as sound waves. The pressure of the air is what moves the ear drum, as the vibrations move the fluid in the cochlea and bend the hair cells, each responding to different frequencies and volume. The ear canal resonates at the same frequency as the larynx. They are partners in sound – just as the listener and speaker are joined by this vibration of air. It's a bridge of energy between us. When we voice we move beyond ourselves into something bigger. When we voice together we create new harmonies.

The confidence you find, the roots you plant, gives you the growth to achieve what Maslow called 'self-transcendence'.[1] (In simple terms this means your ability to get over yourself and to connect out to the world.) Maslow had come to understand that self-actualisation and the confidence it gave people was a transition, a threshold to allow people to step into what he called 'transcendence', where they were able to be in connection, in community, part of something bigger than themselves.[2] The word transcend comes from the Latin *transcendentum*, meaning to surmount, to rise above. Transcendence seems like a necessary rebalancing when we are constantly looking inward and down at our devices when we could be looking up and out at the world around us. A virus can travel around the world in 24 hours. A forest in the Amazon can help rainfall thousands of miles away. Your 'self', your 'personal brand', won't help you when there's no rainfall because the trees have been cut down, or the air you breathe is polluted. There's no *me*, without a connection to the *we* – the communities and living systems we all depend upon.

The transcendence that the voice can give you is practical, rooted and energetic. As you've learned, voice, in its simplest terms, is about *strong back and soft front*. Your strong back gives you an embodied confidence, in the breath, in the spine, in the voice, that enables you to trust in and transcend yourself. Your soft front opens you up to the world, allows you to be light in breath, open in mind, connected and empathetic. The more you let go of your anxieties, the more you listen. The more you let go of your tensions, the more the breath and voice open up. When you befriend your voice, this little human miracle, it anchors you in your body and in your connectedness at the same time – the air you breathe, the ears and brains of others. I'm no physicist, but voice helps me to understand Richard Feynman's famous quote: 'You can't say A is made of B or vice versa. All mass is interaction.'

Try This: Rise Above It

If you ever feel stuck, or need to know how to speak up, or how to find your voice in a way that will connect with others, it can help to take Maslow's advice (see above) and transcend your current state for a moment.

1. Come into the experience of the moment. Connect to your body by pressing your palms together on your diaphragm, one palm pressing into the other. Feel the core strength that lifts as you press, feel how it powers into your voice as you speak.

2. Take a moment now to go forward in time in your mind, perhaps 10, 20, 30 years in the future. Ask the wiser you in the future what advice s/he has for you to help you now. The perspective of looking back in time can help you as it transcends the feelings of the present.

3. Now imagine looking down at the scene from a distance – what do these people need that they haven't seen or heard before? What can you see that you need to do differently? Or you could try imagining experiencing this moment as someone with a completely different perspective. How could it look to them?

When you transcend your own world view you can also rise above the frustrations we all experience when we get locked in our heads. In *The Moment of Lift,* Melinda Gates writes: 'There is a big difference between a loud voice and a strong voice ... strong ... voices for freedom and dignity came from [those] who mastered their pain ... without passing it on. Anyone who can combine those two, finds a voice.'[3]

The ability to transcend, to connect, to listen, is voice on its most powerful level. It's where we find the harmonies rather than competing as a solo act; where we get beyond personal slights and worries to achieve something bigger than we could have imagined.

When our voices come together incredible things can happen. The voice is like water: subtle, fluid, but enormously powerful as a collective force. In 1987, the Estonian people created a revolution as they sang. This 'Singing Revolution' began in the White Nights of summer, when thousands of concertgoers at the Tallinn Festival linked hands and began to sing the patriotic festival songs that had been forbidden during 50 years of Soviet occupation. These songfests and protests continued to build until on 11 September 1988, 300,000 people – almost a quarter of the population – gathered to sing and make a public demand for independence (independence was declared in 1991). As the *New York Times* reported, 'Imagine the scene in *Casablanca* in which the French patrons sing 'La Marseillaise' in defiance of the Germans, then multiply its power by a factor of thousands.'[4]

We only have a short time on earth to express our aliveness. So, why not speak? What are you waiting for? The writer and activist Audre Lorde wrote powerfully about this after a cancer diagnosis:

> In becoming forcibly and essentially aware of my mortality, and of what I wished and wanted for my life, however short it might be, priorities and omissions became strongly etched in a merciless light and what I most regretted were my silences. Of what had I ever been afraid? To question or to speak as I believed could have meant pain or death. But we all hurt in so many different ways, all the time, and pain will either change or end. Death, on the other hand, is the final silence. And that might be coming quickly, now, without regard for whether I had ever spoken what needed to be said, or had only betrayed myself into small silences, while I planned someday to speak, or waited for someone else's words. And I began to recognize a source of power within myself that comes from the knowledge that while it is most desirable not to be afraid, learning to put fear into perspective gave me a great strength. I was going to die, if not sooner then later, whether or not I had ever spoken myself. My silences had not protected me. Your silence will not protect you.[5]

My advice to you? Find your song, and sing it.

Notes

Introduction

1. The Apgar score is used to rate the health of newborns. It takes its name from the doctor who developed it in 1952, Virginia Apgar. The score is based on five criteria: appearance, pulse, grimace, activity, respiration.
2. David Foster Wallace told this story in his Kenyon commencement speech on 21 May 2005; the speech is reproduced in full in *This is Water: Some Thoughts, Delivered on a Significant Occasion, about Living a Compassionate Life* (Little Brown, 2009).
3. Al Alvarez, *The Writer's Voice* (Bloomsbury, 2006), p. 18.
4. Quoted in Simone Stolzoff, 'LinkedIn CEO Jeff Weiner says the biggest skills gap in the US is not coding', *Quartz at Work* (15 October 2018), https://qz.com/work/1423267/linkedin-ceo-jeff-weiner-the-main-us-skills-gap-is-not-coding/, accessed 7 Nov. 2019.
5. Deirdre McCloskey and Arjo Klamer, 'One Quarter of GDP is Persuasion', *American Economic Review*, vol. 85, issue 2 (1995), pp. 191–5.
6. Gerry Antioch, 'Persuasion is now 30 per cent of US GDP', *Economic Roundup*, issue 1 (2013), https://treasury.gov.au/publication/economic-roundup-issue-1-2013/economic-roundup-issue-1-2013/persuasion-is-now-30-per-cent-of-us-gdp, accessed 7 Nov. 2019.

7. Joseph S. Nye, Jr, *Soft Power: The Means To Success in World Politics* (PublicAffairs, 2002).

Chapter One Your Incredible Instrument

1. Caroline Goyder, TEDxBrixton, 'The Surprising Secret to Speaking with Confidence' [video], YouTube (recorded October 2014, uploaded 25 Nov. 2014), https://www.youtube.com/watch?v=a2MR5XbJtXU, accessed 7 Nov. 2019.
2. Antonio Damasio, *The Feeling of What Happens: Body and Emotion in the Making of Consciousness* (Harcourt Brace, 1999), p. 31.
3. For example: Lingua Health, 'Speech-Language Pathology: The Vocal Cords in Action' [video], YouTube (uploaded 5 Dec. 2012), https://www.youtube.com/watch?v=y2okeYVclQo, accessed 7 Nov. 2019.
4. Kristin Linklater, 'The Alchemy of Breathing', in Jane Boston and Rena Cook, eds, *Breath In Action: The Art of Breath in Vocal and Holistic Practice* (Jessica Kingsley Publishers, 2009), p. 105.
5. Jean Hall, *Breathe: Simple Breathing Techniques for a Calmer, Happier Life* (Quadrille, 2016).
6. Donna Farhi, *The Breathing Book* (Henry Holt and Co., 1996).
7. Pierre Philippot, Gaëtane Chapelle and Sylvie Blairy, 'Respiratory Feedback in the Generation of Emotion', *Cognition and Emotion*, vol. 16, issue 5 (2002), pp. 605–27.
8. S. M. Clift and G. Hancox, 'The Perceived Benefits of Singing: Findings From Preliminary Surveys of a University College Choral Society', *Journal of the Royal Society for the Promotion of Health*, vol. 121, issue 4 (2001), pp. 248–56. The University of Frankfurt found that after singing Mozart's *Requiem* for an hour, choir members' blood test results showed significantly increased concentrations of immunoglobulin (proteins in immune system which function as antibodies) and hydrocortisone (an anti-stress hormone).

9. P. S. Holzman and C. Rousey, 'The Voice As a Percept', *Journal of Personality and Social Psychology*, vol. 4, issue 1 (1966), pp. 79–86.

Chapter Two Find Your Calm Centre

1. Linda Stone, 'Are You Breathing? Do You Have Email Apnea?' (24 Nov. 2014), https://lindastone.net/tag/screen-apnea, accessed 7 Nov. 2019.

2. Ibid.

3. I-Mei Lin and Erik Peper, 'Psychophysiological Patterns During Cell Phone Text Messaging: A Preliminary Study', *Applied Psychophysiology and Biofeedback*, vol. 34, issue 1 (2009), pp. 53–7.

4. Marshall McLuhan, *Understanding Media* (Sphere, 1964), p. 53.

5. John Betjeman, 'Slough', 'Tinned fruit, tinned meat, tinned milk, tinned beans, / Tinned minds, tinned breath.' *John Betjeman Collected Poems* (Hodder & Stoughton, 1989).

6. Stephen W. Porges, *The Polyvagal Theory: Neurophysiological Foundations of Emotions, Attachment, Communication and Self-regulation* (W. W. Norton and Company, 2011).

7–8. Bessel van der Kolk, *The Body Keeps the Score: Mind, Brain and Body in the Transformation of Trauma* (Penguin, 2014).

9. Bangalore G Kalyani, Ganesan Venkatasubramanian, Bangalore N Gandaghar et al, 'Neurohemodynamic correlates of 'OM' chanting', *International Journal of Yoga* 2011.

10. Anne Lamott, TED2017, '12 Truths I Learned From Life and Writing' [video], Ted.com (April 2017), https://www.ted.com/talks/anne_lamott_12_truths_i_learned_from_life_and_writing?language=en, accessed 7 Nov. 2019.

11. Simon Annand, *The Half: Photographs of Actors Preparing for the Stage* (Faber, 2008).

Chapter Three Get Out of Your Head

1. Katarzyna Pisanski, Anna Oleszkiewicz, Justyna Plachetka, Marzena Gmiterek and David Reby, 'Voice Pitch Modulation in Human Mate Choice', *Proceedings of the Royal Society B: Biological Sciences*, vol. 285, issue 1893 (Dec. 2018), pp. 1–8.
2. Joan Halifax, *Being With Dying: Cultivating Compassion and Fearlessness in the Presence of Death* (Shambhala Publications, 2009).
3. Helen Russell, *The Atlas of Happiness* (Two Roads, 2018).
4. Richard Llewellyn, *How Green Was My Valley*, quoted in Frankie Armstrong with Jenny Pearson, *As Far as the Eye Can Sing* (Women's Press, 1992), p. 109.
5. Ibid.
6. Bessel van der Kolk, *The Body Keeps the Score: Mind, Brain and Body in the Transformation of Trauma* (Penguin, 2014).
7. Cicely Berry, *Your Voice and How to Use It* (Virgin Books, 1990).
8. Pablo Briñol, Richard E. Petty, Benjamin Wagner, 'Body Posture Effects on Self-evaluation: A Self-validation Approach', *European Journal of Social Psychology*, vol. 39, issue 6 (Oct. 2009), pp. 1053–64.
9. The Text Neck Institute, https://www.text-neck.com/.
10. Adalbert Kapandji, *The Physiology of the Joints, Volume 3*.
11. S. Thomas Scott, 'The Effects of Tactile, Singer-initiated Head and Neck Alignment on Postural, Acoustic, and Perceptual Measures of Male Singers' [oral presentation], University of Kansas Vocal/Choral Pedagogy Research Group (June 2016). In a session of this symposium, Scott presented his research on male singers, finding that if their heads were in correct alignment, as compared to text-neck positioning, they self-reported that they had a better ease of production and, generally, their resonance improved.
12. Jintae Han, Youngju Kim, Soojin Park, Yeonsung Choi, 'Effects of Forward Head Posture on Forced Vital Capacity and

Respiratory Muscles Activity', *Journal of Physical Therapy Science*, vol. 28, issue 1 (Jan. 2016), pp. 128–131.

13. Phil McAleer, Alexander Todorov, Pascal Belin, 'How Do You Say "Hello"? Personality Impressions From Brief Novel Voices', *PLOS ONE* (12 Mar. 2014), https://doi.org/10.1371/journal.pone.0090779

14. Joan Halifax, *Being With Dying: Cultivating Compassion and Fearlessness in the Presence of Death* (Shambhala Publications, 2009).

15. V. Tibbetts and E. Peper, 'Effects of Imagery and Position on Breathing Patterns', *Proceedings of the Twenty-seventh Annual Meeting of the Association for Applied Psychophysiology and Biofeedback* (AAPB, 1996).

16. Nikolaas Tinbergen, 'Ethology and Stress Diseases', Nobel Lecture [video], 12 Dec. 1973, https://www.nobelprize.org/prizes/medicine/1973/tinbergen/lecture/, accessed 7 Nov. 2019.

17. Ibid.

Chapter Four Speak Up and Stand Out

1. Ben Zander (from his talk at the Sage Centre, Newcastle).

2. Viola Spolin, *Theater Games for the Lone Actor: A Handbook* (Northwestern University, 2001).

3. C. Otto Scharmer, *Theory U: Leading from the Future as It Emerges* (Society for Organizational Learning, 2007).

4. kcbaker.com, accessed 7 Nov. 2019.

5. Cicely Berry, *Your Voice and How To Use It* (Virgin, 2000).

Chapter Five Strong Back, Soft Front

1. Abraham Maslow, *The Farther Reaches of Human Nature* (Penguin, 1994).

2. Ibid.

3. Melinda Gates, *The Moment of Lift* (Bluebird, 2019).

4. Matt Zoller Seitz, 'Songs for a Brighter Tomorrow', *New York Times* (14 Dec. 2007), https://www.nytimes.com/2007/12/14/movies/14revo.html, accessed 7 Nov. 2019.
5. Audre Lorde, *Your Silence Will Not Protect You: Essays and Poems* (Silver Press, 2017).

Further Reading

In writing this book I owe a very great debt to the giants of voice and movement (some of whose work you will find listed below), many of whom I have had the good fortune to have been taught by in classes or masterclasses on my MA Voice Studies at Royal Central School of Speech and Drama.

When my publishers asked me to change the title of this book from 'Get Out Of Your Head' to *Find Your Voice*, I worried enormously because one of the books that was utterly essential to me as a voice student was Barbara Houseman's genius book *Finding Your Voice*. It's a wonderful book to introduce you to the world of voice for professional actors and will add so much depth to the fundamentals we have covered here. I cannot recommend it highly enough.

I invite you to explore further and follow your curiosity. Voice is a path which will never cease to enrich you if you keep exploring.

Armstrong, Frankie, *As Far As the Eye Can Sing* (The Women's Press, 1992).
Berry, Cicely, *Voice and The Actor* (Virgin, 2000).
Berry, Cicely, *Your Voice and How To Use It* (Virgin, 2000).

Carey, David and Clark Carey, Rebecca, *The Vocal Arts Workbook* (Methuen Drama, 2008).

Groskop Viv, *How To Own The Room* (Bantam Press, 2018).

Houseman, Barbara, *Finding Your Voice* (Nick Hern Books, 2002).

Karpf, Anne, *The Human Voice* (Bloomsbury, 2007).

Linklater, Kristin, *Freeing the Natural Voice* (Drama Publishers, 2006).

McCallion, Michael, *The Voice Book* (rev. ed., Faber & Faber Ltd, 1998).

Acknowledgements

My thanks to:

My teachers at Royal Central School of Speech and Drama and beyond – voice, Pilates, Alexander technique. We teach what we need and over the last 25 years you have all supported me with inspiration, a bit of tough love and practical feedback to get out of my head and find my voice. I've got so much to learn still, and relish it every day. You are masters of your craft.

Sam Jackson for commissioning the book. Your ongoing support and belief is transformative. Thank you also for honest feedback when required, I appreciate it.

Becky Alexander for being brilliantly supportive, kind and thoughtful in the edit process – you have made all the difference. Addy – for your help in getting this book out there!

Viktorija Semjonova for your beautiful illustrations, and Clare Hubbard for essential and incisive copy editing – massively appreciated.

Jonny Geller, Catherine Cho, Alice Lutyens and the team at Curtis Brown – thank you for having my back!

There were a few midwives of this book at different stages: Chloe Fox – for your brilliant support and wise words – it meant a lot to me; Caroline Donald for help with early chapters; Amy Gadney for inspiration and being a fellow traveller on a sometimes lonely road!

Stephanie Busari, Denise Graveline (much missed), Chris Head and George McCallum (creator of the chest of drawers!) because you were so key in my TEDx journey which is the foundation of this book.

Debbie, Fatima, Gueddy, Sarah – for your patience in holding the fort! Couldn't have done it without you.

Brendan, Amelia, Lucy, Katie at London Business Forum for your belief in the book and brilliance in what you do.

My family and friends. It's only when you emerge from writing a book that you realise how much it possesses you in the writing. Apologies for the last year everyone, normal service is about to resume!

Neeve – I hope you write your book one day too. Keep reading them.

This book is about how you build your voice from the ground up, the roots you plant and how they sustain you. It's also about the air we breathe. If you care about the air we breathe, then plant trees where you can and join me in giving to the World Land Trust (worldlandtrust.org) who buy, restore and protect rainforests across the globe. There is little more important this century than to ensure that we plant more trees – and there is no better way to do that than to give to the World Land Trust. In the words of David Attenborough: 'The money that is given to the World Land Trust, in my estimation, has more effect on the wild world than almost anything I can think of. The World Land Trust, in my estimation, is leading the way.'

*

'Another world is not only possible, she is on her way. On a quiet day, I can hear her breathing.'

Arundhati Roy

About Caroline Goyder

Caroline's global reputation as a speaker and voice coach is built on her warm, engaging, relaxed and highly practical style, and her expertise honed by her work with actors, teachers, broadcasters and the corporate sector. She worked for many years at Royal Central School of Speech and Drama as a voice coach. Her skill is to take ideas previously known by performers and broadcasters and to make them immediately usable for the audience in their personal and professional challenges. She is regularly sought after by the media as an expert in her field and her work has featured on television and in numerous national and international newspaper articles. Her TED Talk (https://www.youtube.com/watch?v=a2MR5Xb JtXU) on speaking with confidence has had many millions of views. At Caroline's website (carolinegoyder.com) you will find information about booking Caroline to speak and signing up for her 'Find Your Voice' events. You can also download short audio courses to help you speak with confidence.

You can find Caroline across social media: @Carolinegoyder

Index

Page references in *italics* indicate images.

'abracadabra' 4
accents 49–50, 53, 194
adrenalin 4, 69, 73, 76, 77, 80, 83, 84, 85,
    100, 156, 196, 201
Alexander technique 127, 138, 139–40, 144
Alvarez, Al 2
Angelou, Maya 41; *Rainbow in the Cloud*
    105, 115
Annand, Simon 96
Apgar score 1
Aristotle 11
articulators/articulation 24, 25, 26, 26, 52–4,
    52, 60, 62, 193, 194
autonomic nervous system (ANS) 66, 69–70,
    75–87, 90, 91, 103, 104, 149, 196, 197

back, strong 106, 116, 120, 122–3, 126,
    127–9, 144, 202, 204
Baker, KC 167
Beaton, Cecil 20
beliefs, writing down your 168
Berry, Cicely: *Your Voice and How to Use it*
    Successfully vi, 90, 117, 194
Big Ted (large chest of drawers shaped like a
    man's torso) 23–4, 24, 25
blank, going 2, 9, 78–9, 80, 84, 102
blushing/flushing 65, 84, 100, 101
body 4, 9, 26, 26, 62, 105–44, 201–2
  Be in Your Body exercise 110–11
  confident voices and 105–44
  'getting out of your head' and 108–11,
    137, 201–2

instrument of voice/how your voice works
    and 23–63, 24, 25, 26, 28, 31, 34, 36,
    39, 44, 46, 52, 55
interoception (bringing attention into the
    body) 109–11
loving your voice and 111–15
mind, body and voice, link between 10,
    12, 109, 200
posture and 115–44 *see also* posture
questions concerning 142–3
relaxed 129–38 *see also* relaxed body
body language 38, 160, 185
boldness 55–6, 146, 179, 185, 195, 199, 202
'born' speaker 4, 5
breath:
  Are You Holding Your Breath? exercise
    73–4, 100
  buzzing bee breath 95–6, 103, 178
  daily attention to 36–8, 36
  devices and 70, 72, 73–4, 104, 123, 124,
    125
  diaphragm and *see* diaphragm
  Feel the Reflex exercise 34–5, 34
  feet on the ground and 130–1
  Find Your Roots exercise 132
  gasp and 87–90, 88, 99–100, 190, 201
  half and 97–8
  holding your 9, 70, 73–4, 95, 100, 104,
    123, 124, 196
  instrument of voice and (hitter) 25, 26,
    26, 27, 31–46, 31, 34, 36, 39, 44, 62,
    201